DESERT EAGLES

DESERT EAGLES

HUMPHREY WYNN

An Airlife
CLASSIC

Copyright © 1993 Humphrey Wynn

First published in the UK in 1993
by Airlife Publishing Ltd

This edition published 2001

British Library Cataloguing-in-Publication Data
  A catalogue record for this book
  is available from the British Library

ISBN 1 84037 293 1

Printed in England by St Edmundsbury Press Ltd, Bury St Edmunds, Suffolk

Airlife Publishing Ltd
101 Longden Road, Shrewsbury, SY3 9EB, England
E-mail: airlife@airlifebooks.com
Website: www.airlifebooks.com

Dedicated to the gallant memory of
Hal Marting MC
and to
Michael Miluck
of Genoa, Nevada, USA;
also to all ex-aircrew and ground crew
members of No 239 Wing, Desert Air Force, and
its squadrons — Nos 3 (RAAF), 112, 250 and 450 (RAAF)

Contents

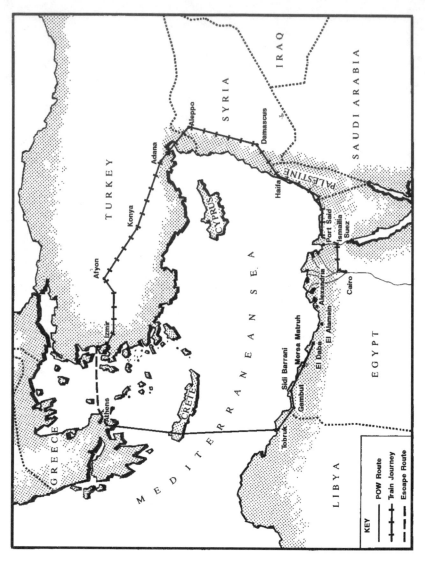

Hal Marting's journeys as a PoW, as an escaper/evader and en route to Cairo from Western Turkey. While his initial journey after he was captured at El Daba, and his train journey through Turkey, Syria and Palestine to Egypt, are well documented, there is no detailed information as to where he went while "on the run" in Greece, nor as to exactly where he crossed the Aegean Sea, so the routes shown are approximations.

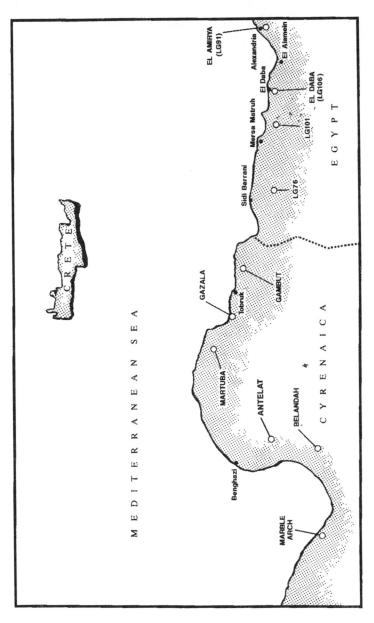

Landing-grounds used by the Kittyhawk squadrons of No 239 Wing during their advance in support of the 8th Army, as mentioned in the text.

Acknowledgements

To Michael Miluck for a copy of his No 250 Sqn diary and wartime photographs; to Chester D. Silvers for information on the late Hal Marting's family; and to Mrs Nancy Miluck for obtaining a copy of his diary and other material from his sister, the late Lenore Silvers, and for her indefatigable correspondence and boundless enthusiasm for the Eagle squadrons, their personnel and their history. Also to my friends in the Air Historical Branch, Ministry of Defence: Leslie Howard, Eric Munday, Harry Naraine and Richard Knight, for all their help in the matter of ORBs, maps and other information relating to the Desert Air Force and finally to Graham Meadowcroft for his sketch-maps and Eric Bullen for his photographs of the Marting diaries and RAF/USAAF documents.

H.W.

Preface

Some years ago a good American friend, Michael Miluck, presented me with four Second World War diaries — his own, a typed version of his daily notes describing the air fighting before, during and after the Battle of El Alamein in October 1942; and three others belonging to a wartime friend of his, Hal Marting: a brown-covered one with a clasp, covering the whole of 1942 and with an Eagle squadrons' badge stuck inside its end pages; a red-covered one, bought in South Africa and with entries dating from 18 May to 26 October 1942 (dates whose significance will subsequently become clear); and a small, dark blue-covered Turkish one — the reason for which will, again, be revealed later.

Edward (as he then was)* Miluck and Hal Marting were both US volunteers who flew with the Eagle squadrons (three of which were formed — Nos 71, 121 and 133) in RAF Fighter Command in 1941. During 1942 most of these American fighter pilots were absorbed into the US Army Air Force in Britain and flew P-51 Mustangs, P-47 Thunderbolts or P-38 Lightnings; but some of them stayed in the RAF and went out to Malta or the Middle East, and Miluck and Marting were posted to the latter theatre, to P-40 Kittyhawk squadrons in No 239 Wing just prior to the Battle of El Alamein.

What happened to them was recorded in their diaries and forms the basis of this book, the author of which (who also served in that theatre of war at that time) has done his best to recreate the atmosphere of the crucial battle which was one of the turning-points of the Second World War — based on their personal experiences which they set down at the time.

He is very grateful to have had the privilege of doing this.

H.W.
October 1992

---

* He changed his Christian name to Michael in 1947.

Prologue

Egypt in July 1942, when the two ex-Eagle squadron pilots arrived there, was in the front line in the Second World War — at a time which saw the nadir of Allied fortunes: German Armies were within striking distance of Moscow and Alexandria and besieging Leningrad and Stalingrad.

Britain's 8th Army in the Western Desert had halted Germany's Afrika Korps and Italy's Divisions at a bottleneck about 30 miles wide, with the Mediterranean Sea on one flank and the Qattara Depression on the other, about 40 miles from Alexandria: all was set for a great battle, victory in which would drive the Allies westwards and the German/Italian Armies back towards Tripoli. Defeat, for the Allies, was unthinkable: they had to win this time. The Battle of El Alamein, when it occurred in October 1942, was to be one of the decisive encounters of the Second World War.

Meanwhile the 8th Army and the Desert Air Force were like a great coiled spring, ready to be released, strengthened day by day with reinforcements of men and materiel: tanks, guns, aircraft, ammunition, fuel, food and water — that most precious commodity in the desert.

All this build-up was occurring in Egypt — that ancient land depending entirely on the Nile river, with its Delta spreading out towards the Mediterranean — a green and fertile area flanked by deserts to the west and east. The Delta area, with the great port of Alexandria at its head and the city of Cairo to the south, was itself largely untouched by the war: in its cultivated acres the fellahin — the Egyptian peasantry — pursued their tasks of irrigated farming as they had done for centuries, and would continue to do so, had the Germans and Italians successfully invaded.

The Allied military deployment in Egypt had its headquarters in Cairo and Alexandria but used the desert areas: a key road was the military one between the two cities — out from Cairo towards the Pyramids at Mena, then north-westwards, a black line of tarmac with the Western Desert on its western side and the Delta to the east. At its northern end this road forked on the edge of the blue Mediterranean — to the right for Alexandria, to the left for El Alamein. On both sides of the road were airfields — some with tarmac runways, most of them just stretches of sand, their boundaries marked by oil drums.

The Desert Air Force, which Marting and Miluck were soon to join in time for the decisive battle at El Alamein and the advance westwards, was based on these airfields within reach of the Cairo–Alexandria road and on those on the other side of the Delta: the day fighters, fighter-bombers and medium bombers (Spitfires, Hurricanes, Kittyhawks, Bostons, Baltimores and B-25 Mitchells) were all within range of the Army's positions; the night fighters and heavy bombers (Beaufighters, Wellingtons, Halifaxes and B-24 Liberators) further back, on the eastern side of the Delta; and the anti-shipping/anti-submarine squadrons – Beaufighters, Beauforts and Sunderlands — in the area of Alexandria and on the coastline to its east.

On the eastern side of the Delta were the ports at the northern and southern ends of the Suez Canal — Port Said and Port Tewfiq. And it was from the latter that the two young Americans got their first glimpse of Egypt when their troopship *Nieuw Amsterdam* anchored there at the end of the 12-day voyage from Durban, on 9 July 1942.

They had been in South Africa since 18 May, waiting for transport to the Middle East, spending their time golfing and swimming — so they were both very fit.

CHAPTER 1

To Africa

Tall buildings on the horizon. This was the first sight of Durban — and of Africa — for Flying Officers Hal Marting and Edward Miluck, from the deck of the troopship *Aorangi*. It was 18 May 1942, and they had left England early in April.

Only eleven months before Miluck had seen Europe for the first time, when he arrived at Liverpool aboard the *Georgic* from Halifax, NS. Marting had crossed the Atlantic in HMS *Derbyshire*, sailing from Halifax on 30 May and reaching Greenock on 28 June 1941.

During their six-week voyage to South Africa in a convoy that had lost a merchantman and had an escorting naval vessel damaged between West Africa and the Cape[1], the two young Americans had had plenty of time to reflect on what had happened to them so far, and to speculate on what was to come.

Marting, just 31, was a good deal older than most of his fellow-pilots and had a great deal of military experience before the Second World War. Born in Eckerty, Indiana, on 1 March 1911, 'kid brother' to seven elder sisters, he had left school at 18 to join the US Marines and took part in their operations in Haiti in 1929. He was thus a tough, well-trained soldier long before he became an airman, and this background was to help him in his experiences in the Middle East and afterwards — especially his escape from captivity.

He came out of the Marines in 1931 and, back in civilian life, learned to fly; then in 1940 he was considered too old for flying duties in the Army Air Corps. So he joined the RCAF — and was sworn-in in Vancouver, BC, on 10 October 1940, and trained at Regina, Saskatchewan (ITS), Windsor, Ontario (EFTS), Dunnesville, Ontario (SFS) and Trenton, Ontario (CFS)[2], getting his wings on 29 March 1941 and being commissioned as Pilot Officer.

Miluck's background was a boyhood in Mandan, North Dakota, where he was born in 1918. He had won a basketball scholarship at the University of North Dakota, then after two and a half years of liberal arts studies, he won a US Army Air Corps cadetship, graduating at Santa Maria, California. From there he was sent to Randolph Field, San Antonio, Texas, but was disqualified in flying training — something which happened to many others who later became successful operational pilots. It was 1940 and he was 21. He had done 120 hours' flying.

The chance came to join the RAF, through the Clayton Knight Committee[3]: he enlisted and sailed from Halifax, NS, to Liverpool in February 1941 — not, as he was to recall in later years, to help to make the world safe for democracy or for any other such lofty ideals: he wanted to fly aircraft, to see the world and have adventures; he was a young man, from a rural area, who wanted to get away.

Both Marting and Miluck had gone through RAF operational training in the UK — Marting at No 59 OTU, Crosby, and Longtown, Cumberland, and Miluck at No 56 OTU, Sutton Bridge in Lincolnshire, on Hurricanes in the spring of 1941. They both joined No 121 Sqn, the second Eagle squadron of American volunteers to be formed, in August 1941 at Kirton-in-Lindsey, Lincolnshire. Both also served in No 71 Sqn, the first Eagle squadron to be formed.

What brought them together on a troopship bound for Egypt was a request for a posting to the Far East — they had hoped to join the Flying Tigers of General Claire Chennault's Air Force in that theatre. It had become known in the Eagle squadrons that they were to be transferred to the US Army Air Force, which occurred in September 1942. (Marting and Miluck, together with two other ex-Eagle squadron pilots, Flying Officers Mike Kelly and Wally Tribken, all did later join the USAAF.)[4]

SS *Aorangi* docked in Durban at about 1300hr on 18 May; she had passed through a harbour filled with shipping and edged her way to the dockside in an inner harbour; but it was dark before her 'troops' could get off — glad to feel solid ground under their feet after the heaving and dangerous discomforts of their long voyage. They were in Africa at last, operational experience in Europe behind them, bound for the limbo of a military transit camp before the second part of their voyage.

In the darkness of that mid-May evening, Marting and Miluck, with hundreds of other RAF personnel, got aboard a troop train at the dockside: their destination – Clarewood Transit Camp, a tented city outside Durban, temporary home for some 13,000 military personnel — an indication of the huge build-up of troops before the Allies' final desert offensive. By the time the new draft got there, there was a serious shortage of accommodation: in any case, the best that Clarewood could offer was two to a tent, the occupants sleeping on the ground with only a thin mattress and a blanket.

Marting decided that this wasn't for him: so with Wing Commander Tyson and Squadron Leader Bangs he went into Durban, where they booked in at the Federal Hotel, Marting sharing a room with the squadron leader. What he couldn't get used to after the London black-out was the lights coming on at night — they seemed to burn his eyes. The second surprise was the amount of food of all kinds which was available after the rationing of wartime Britain: they discovered this over a leisurely breakfast, having begun their first day in Durban with a cup of coffee brought in by an African boy.

It was to be the first of thirty-nine days in Durban — days spent in the sunshine, just filling in time and keeping fit. On that first morning, however, they went back to Clarewood Transit Camp to try to find their luggage — which had not arrived; and the camp itself looked even worse in the daylight, so they returned to Durban, which Marting thought 'a lovely place — just like most American cities', and the weather 'just like southern California'.

Day then succeeded day until almost the end of June — shopping first ('there seem to be no shortages except in gasoline, golf balls and light bulbs') for sports shirts, slacks, sandals, socks, underwear and toilet articles and 'something to send Marilyn[5] — an ivory bracelet and hand-carved necklace'; swimming almost every day — in the sea or in a salt-water pool on the beach ('the water was 70° and just right'); sightseeing ('Tribken and I went down to the native market this afternoon' — this was on 23 May — 'and took several pictures which should be good'); sampling Durban's night life ('went to the Stardust Night Club with Miluck and another American, Pat Wilson. Got a little tight but didn't have much fun'); going to the races ('Miluck and I won a pound each and had a very good time'); golfing at the Durban Country Club ('very fine...and one of the most beautiful courses I've ever seen'); and dating girls ('tonight' — this was on 29 May — 'Miluck and I took two girls from Johannesburg out dancing. Had a nice time. Stopped in at the Doll's House for a real American milk shake and toasted sandwich'.) They even heard a speech by the South African Prime Minister, Field Marshal JC Smuts. For this purpose there was a parade on 3 June, at which Marting commanded a flight. The troops formed up and entrained that morning at Clarewood Transit Camp; from the train they 'marched about ten blocks to the park', Smuts arriving there at 1215hr. In the event there seems to have been something of an anticlimax: Smuts 'made a short speech of very little importance and the parade was over by 1300hr'. As Marting 'didn't have to take the men back to camp' he stayed in Durban for lunch.

Meanwhile there was a movement out of Clarewood: on 25 May Marting noted that 'nearly all the troops are gone now. All but about 20 of us who were on the *Aorangi* left today. Don't know how long we will be here'.

In fact, another month of shopping, going to the races, dating girls, swimming and golfing lay ahead — the golf including rounds with the legendary South African player Bobby Locke, the first on 20 June at the Country Club:

> This afternoon Jack Hex and I played Bobby Locke and Ike Williams who is a scratch golfer. They gave us four up and we beat them four and three. My game was clicking and my putts were OK....

It was through his golf that Marting got into the air again. On the 25th he played with Colonel Wilmot, CO of the local

SAAF station and 'arranged for a flip in a Harvard tomorrow morning'. But this was almost too late, for the Americans had heard that they were on the move at last: 'Just got word tonight that we are to leave tomorrow and I am supposed to be out at camp by 0900hr which is impossible for me. Am getting packed now.'

But he was in luck, for there was a 24-hour postponement of their departure. On the 26th

> Col Wilmot came by the hotel for me at 0830hr and I went to the aerodrome with him. He loaned me his car and chauffeur to pick up my baggage and take us out to camp. Got out there about 1030hr only to discover we are leaving tomorrow instead of today so came back into town and had a 30-minute flip in a Harvard[6] before brunch. Had brunch at the Country Club and "18" with the Colonel afterwards....

The Americans marked the end of their enforced stay in Durban appropriately: 'Got tight this evening and went to the Cosmo Club with Miluck. We spent the night in Gladys Myles' apartment (she is one of the managers of the club) and she stayed with her sister.'

Next day (27 June) they were on their way to Egypt and the desert war.

> Gladys woke us at 0645hr and we hiked out to camp, arriving at 0800hr, just in time to get our baggage out and get ready to leave. Went by train to the docks and were aboard the *Nieuw Amsterdam* by 1200hr. We sailed about two. I slept all afternoon because I was dead tired.

Nevertheless they were all fit for whatever lay ahead: the fresh air, the sunshine, the exercise and the good food they had had in South Africa had reinvigorated them; and the five-day voyage to Egypt was to be trouble-free compared with the anxieties and battles of their convoy through the

Atlantic from Britain to South Africa. Their accommodation, too, was much better:

'This ship is a beauty', Marting recorded on their first day at sea (Saturday, 27 June). 'Tribken, Kelly and myself have a cabin with private bath and it is very nice. This is a first-class liner and is in good shape. We are travelling alone — no escort — and must be doing about 20 knots.'

'Travelling alone — no escort...'. The long days of the Atlantic convoys, with the ever-present threat of U-boat attacks, were already just another grim wartime memory; for almost a week Marting, Miluck and the other military personnel aboard travelled almost like peacetime cruise passengers — out into the Indian Ocean, then northwards to the Red Sea, towards the heat and the desert sands of Egypt.

At first the weather was fresh. 'We have been heading east most of the day', Marting recorded on Sunday, 28 June. 'The weather is clear but pretty windy and this ship pitches and rolls all over the ocean. She is quite large — 36,000 tons — but she sure rolls just the same. Have started making a square knot cartridge belt. Spent most of the day doing that and reading....

By the following day the wind had abated; the ship was 'not rolling so badly now but enough'. In their enforced leisure aboard they had obviously been discussing their ultimate destination: 'We are all wondering where we are going. The news from Egypt looks bad, and if we are going to Cairo, we wonder if we will be there in time for the evacuation!'

At that date, Rommel's Afrika Korps were well into Egypt: they had reached Mersa Matruh and were pushing on towards El Alamein: nothing, it seemed, could stop them finally routing the 8th Army and taking Alexandria and Cairo, the keys to the Middle East.

On 30 June, now heading north-eastwards, *Nieuw Amsterdam* was 'riding with the swells — so the rolling isn't bad at all now. Surprisingly enough, none have been seasick yet'. Marting was 'on guard as security officer', but as that entailed 'practically no duties' he was able to go on working on his cartridge belt, which was almost finished.

By 1 July the ship had eased on to a more northerly course and the weather was still good. Marting had finished his belt and had it washed and drying; he was invited to the OC Troops' cabin for drinks before dinner, and in the evening Tribken, Miluck and himself tried to answer questions from *Information Please* — a quiz programme based on the wartime US radio show of that name hosted by Clifton Fadiman and considered to be "the grandfather of all quiz shows".

By the 2nd *Nieuw Amsterdam* was heading north and a little west, making for the Gulf of Aden. 'It looks like we are still going to Cairo', Marting noted in his diary. 'The news from there still looks bad.' In fact, by now the Axis armies were at El Alamein, gateway to the Nile Delta and the rich prize of Egypt.

Increasing heat and blacking-out of the ship's lights for her security in the hours of darkness caused problems of discomfort for some of her passengers: 'It's getting very difficult for most of the fellows to sleep at night now because it's getting pretty warm and with the blackout there is very little ventilation', commented Marting on the 3rd, adding cheerfully: 'It doesn't bother me much. Played cards nearly all day and won four quid. We are still going north. Weather is good.'

On 4th July, US Independence Day, the Americans laid on an appropriate celebration:

> Kelly, Tribken, Miluck and myself threw a party for our friends (about 30) in the lounge this evening. We got properly sloshed and Tribken passed out early after dinner. We celebrated 'The Fourth' in fine fashion as these English expected us to. The party ended with Kelly, Miluck and I making a loud attempt at *The Star-Spangled Banner* accompanied by a Scottish pianist who didn't even know the tune.

For Tribken the party had a less happy ending: a large fellow (weighing over 14 stone), when he was sick in the cabin it took four of his friends to get him along to the toilet. As Marting neatly put it: 'We had a large time looking after Tribken in the cabin.'

But a new day, a new week (it was a Sunday, 5 July) helped to heal all: Marting woke early and the cool shower he had made his head 'feel a bit smaller', and breakfast helped. Meanwhile *Nieuw Amsterdam* was changing course and the heat was increasing:

> We had a concert tonight, which was very good, but it was so hot in the crowded lounge the sweat poured off everyone. We have turned south-west so I guess we are in the Gulf of Aden.

However, they were not to see the famous port — maritime gateway to Arabia for centuries: 'We passed Aden sometime during the night', Marting recorded on the 6th, 'and woke up this morning in the straits between the Gulf of Aden and the Red Sea. It was our first sight of Arabia' — *Nieuw Amsterdam* was proceeding through the narrow entrance into the Red Sea, the misty outline of the Yemen on her starboard side and of Abyssinia to port: 'It is quite hot and the sea is very calm. It is hazy so we can't tell how far we are from land on either side.'

Steadily northwards now, with Egypt on their port side: 'This Red Sea is very calm, very hot and very hazy,' Marting recorded on Tuesday the 7th. 'The ship has slowed down considerably so I think we are ahead of schedule. We are due in at some small port near Suez on Thursday morning.'

There was one day more to go on board and, as a reminder that they were once more in a war zone, air-raid precautions were taken: on the 8th Marting 'was on watch as aircraft spotter for four hours today. We are getting up in range of Jerry's 'planes now and they put the pilots on watch just in case. Didn't see anything.'

On the morning of Thursday, 9 July, the throbbing of *Nieuw Amsterdam*'s engines ceased:

We anchored at Port Tewfiq at about eight this morning. The harbour is filled with all kinds of ships. Went ashore in lighters about ten-thirty and boarded a train for the camp where we will go first.

Marting and Miluck were at last in Egypt. Over three months since they had left England and the war in Europe, here they were joining thousands of other Allied Servicemen in the vast military build-up that was like a great coiled spring, to be released at El Alamein on 23-24 October.[7] After the long throbbing days in a ship it was at least a change to look out of the windows of a train on to Egypt's sandy wastes. For three hours they travelled through them, northwards from Suez to Kasfareet on the Great Bitter Lake: here there was an airfield with black tarmac runways — one of several along the western shore of the lake — and also No 21 Personnel Transit Centre. 'Our quarters are not bad', Marting assessed their new surroundings in his diary. 'Brick houses, two in each and we use our camp kits for beds. Going to bed early tonight as I am pretty tired.'

10 July 1942 was their first day under the cloudless Egyptian skies, and the Americans lost no time in getting to the centre of things — Cairo. On that morning they were up early, and after changing their English money into the local currency (piastres) hitch-hiked into the noisy capital city, booking into its most famous hotel — Shepheard's[8] — and doing some shopping that afternoon for KD (khaki drill) items, universal wear in that hot and reliable climate. Inevitably they encountered old friends in the hotel, a meeting place for Service officers: 'ran into Bob Mannix tonight.... He is in 127 Sqn, flying Hurricanes. They are in action every day.'[9]

Would the newly arrived Americans be flying Hurricanes again or Spitfires or Kittyhawks (Curtiss P-40s)? It was to be nearly another week before they knew. Meanwhile Cairo was the centre of their activities — 'certainly a dirty place and there isn't much to do except drink', Marting wrote on the 11th, noting that he had 'moved out of Shepheard's because of the expense' and was staying at the RAF rest house, Wellington House, in the Mobilia Building: 'it is the top floor of the tallest building in town and from my room I can see the Pyramids'. This view of those symbols of ancient Egypt would have elated many a peacetime tourist, but Marting had other — military — matters on his mind.

After lunch at Wellington House the Americans hitch-hiked out to their transit camp at Kasfareet, only to discover there that they had been posted to another one, No 22 PTC at Almaza near Cairo — 'a pretty awful place'. Marting decided he would stay on at Wellington House — 'as long as I can get away with it'.

His views on Cairo, like those of most Servicemen at that time, were mixed: there seemed to be no shortages there — plenty of food and cigarettes, petrol unrationed. Again he commented on its dirtiness, and the natives were 'incredibly dishonest'; even so it was 'very interesting' but 'the last place I would ever want to live in'. It was 'quite hot here now'.

By now his colleagues were on the move from there: 'Kelly, Tribken and Miluck are all posted to another camp halfway to Alexandria', he noted on Monday, 13 July. 'Don't know why I wasn't sent with them.'

Missing his friends, he went out to Almaza, but there was nothing doing there; so he went to Gezira — a green island in the Nile, near the centre of Cairo, where the Gezira Sporting Club facilities were available to Service officers — and played golf: 'didn't play very well but I was mostly practising and the clubs I had were terrible'. Still staying at Wellington House, he went out to Gezira again the following day, played 18 holes and went swimming afterwards — 'enjoyed it very much'.

But he was impatient to get into action and 'pretty fed up' with what he called the 'red tape and stupidity of the English', so on 15 July took himself off to the American Legation to see about joining the US Army Air Corps. A Colonel who interviewed him 'talked very promisingly' and Marting made an application to transfer, 'but it may be some time before it goes through.'

He played golf again that afternoon at Gezira and when he went back to Wellington House for dinner found he had been posted 'somewhere'. He was to be at Almaza by eight o'clock the following morning.

Notes to Chapter 1

1   See *Angels 22 — A Self Portrait of a Fighter Pilot* by George Barclay, edited by Humphrey Wynn (Arrow Books 1971). Barclay, CO of 601 Squadron, went out in the same convoy with his squadron.

2   Successive Flying Training Schools: Initial (ITS), Elementary (EFTS), Service (SFS), Central (CFS).

3   Official organization in the USA for the recruitment of Americans into the RAF.

4   Tribken was killed in Belgium in 1944 in a jeep accident. Kelly, like Miluck, survived the war, but died in 1986. Marting lost his life in a flying accident in September 1943 in South Carolina: see the Epilogue, p.132.

5   Marting's daughter, then about five years old.

6   North American AT-6 Harvard, a two-seat radial-engined monoplane trainer.

7   But the fighting in the air was going on all the time and the speed with which ex-UK personnel joined it varied: Squadron Leader George Barclay, who was at Clarewood Transit Camp for only five days (19–24 May), re-embarked in HMT *Mauretania* on the 25th and disembarked at Port Tewfiq on 4 June. By the 19th, No 601 Sqn was ready to move into the Western Desert. But the movement, of course, involved a whole squadron: the Americans had been posted to the Middle East as individuals.

8   Haunt of expatriates and tourists for generations, but destined to be burned down during anti-British riots in the 1950s.

9   Sadly Sqn Ldr RL Mannix was killed in action on 18 November 1942. He was then OC No 33 Sqn, having been posted from No 127 at the end of October.

No 250 Squadron; Sqn Ldrs 'Aly' Barber (left) and 'Johnnie' Walker
with Fg Off Ed Miluck.

Sqn Ldr 'Bob' Mannix.

A pre-flight briefing.

An Allied squadron: Plt Off Collier (Canadian), Sgt Nitz (USA),
Fg Off Colver (British) and Plt Off Kopperud (Norwegian) on readiness.

CHAPTER 2
Into the Desert

When he got to Almaza the following morning, it was to learn he'd been posted 'to another transit camp in the Western Desert halfway to Alex.'. This was Wadi Natrun, a sand airfield on the fringe of the Western Desert, just east of the Cairo–Alexandria military road and about halfway between the two cities. Marting left Almaza in a truck at about 0930hr and got to his destination three hours later. The three other Eagles — Kelly, Tribken and Miluck — were all there, but were being posted and were leaving 'right after lunch', so Marting asked to go with them and was posted immediately: he 'didn't even have to unpack'. They found themselves

> about 15 miles south of Alexandria at No 239 Wing[1] where we are to get about ten hours' practice on Kittyhawks. We're right in the middle of nowhere, living in tents and rationed to one canteen of water per day for drinking, washing and everything. The only answer is not to shave or wash.

Their desert service had begun, on 16 July 1942. But, being still near enough to 'civilization', there were some compensations:

> I understand we can go swimming every afternoon so I intend to shave and bathe in Cairo in the afternoons.

No 239 Wing formed part of the fighter/bomber element of the Desert Air Force: it consisted of four squadrons of Kittyhawks — Nos 3 and 450 (RAAF), 112 and 250 (Sudan) Sqn, RAF, and was part of the 'coiled spring' of the Allied forces waiting to be released when the break-out from El Alamein began.[2] Meanwhile there was to be another battle — that of Alam Halfa, beginning at the end of August: had the Axis armies won that one, the road to Alexandria, only 60 miles away, would have lain open to them; but the Allied lines held, and this victory was the key to the greater one which was to come at the end of October.

In the meantime the Americans, as newcomers to the theatre, were getting acclimatized and training for their operational role, though there were some problems:

> Life in the desert is certainly no picnic [Marting noted in his diary on 17 July.] Even if we can go into town and swim every day here, it is unusual. The food is generally pretty bad and consists mostly of bully beef. On the front-line airfields they get very little except that and hard tack. We are very lucky here and get an egg nearly every morning and some green vegetables. Sand and dust get into everything. I can feel it in my teeth all day and night. It is in all the food and even the beer tastes dusty. The floor of our tent is soft sand and of course it is all over all of our clothes and blankets. There is a sand/dust storm every day about six and that is uncomfortable too.

Shortage of aircraft was another problem, owing to unavailability[3] or to accidents: 'They are very short of 'planes here, as they have been nearly everywhere I've been', commented Marting on the 18th. 'Ed Miluck got to fly about 40 minutes in a Hurricane this morning but none of the rest of us got up.'

> One of the fellows already flying Kittyhawks made a bad landing while we were watching. He put the undercarriage out of commission when he hit but got off the ground again, only to find that only one leg worked. Coming in for a belly landing he must have been excited, he made a very poor job of it and washed-out the aircraft. He was very lucky to get out unhurt.

The new pilots of No 239 Wing had to get used to Kittyhawks — which, unlike the British fighters, had toe-activated brakes (instead of a brake lever on the control column) and a tail-wheel which could unlock if the aircraft got into a swing and the pilot over-corrected; for this reason, wheel landings — instead of three-pointers — were practised. On 19 July Marting 'finally got up for 35 minutes this morning in a Harvard practising wheel landings' and 'didn't have any trouble'. Likewise he 'didn't have any trouble' when he flew a Kittyhawk for an hour before breakfast on the 21st and liked it 'pretty well', commenting: 'It isn't nearly as good as a Spit but better than the Hurricane.'

However, he had a 'prang' himself on the 22nd, when he 'wangled' a trip in a Tomahawk (Curtiss-built, precursor of the Kittyhawk) and did some practice landings then took it to Helwan, an airfield south of Cairo with black tarmac runways, the base of No 132 Maintenance Unit, 'to pick up a radiator cooler for one of the other 'planes'. When he got into the circuit at Helwan he found that it was 'a small field' and that there were 'a lot of wogs' — i.e. Egyptian labourers — 'working on one end of the runway'. As a result he overshot:

> I had to come in high to clear them and then brake quite a bit at the end. My right brake grabbed and I ground-looped, dragging the right wing tip and breaking the undercart. They came over and picked me up in the Harvard [North American AT-6 Texan, a two-seat trainer] this evening.

No 239 Wing, busy with its operations, couldn't spare aircraft for the conversion training of new pilots. On 23 July Marting wrote in his diary:

> They were short of 'planes this morning so I didn't get to fly [in fact the Wing did 83 sorties that day — 24 by 3 Sqn, 22 by 112, 18 by 250 and 19 by 450]. Thumbed into town at noon and am staying at Wellington House again tonight. Went swimming at Gezira this afternoon and had a few drinks with the gang tonight.

Clearly Marting and Miluck were dissatisfied with their progress in getting into Desert Air Force operations, so on the 24th they 'went up to the American Legation ... and filled up an application for the US Naval Air Force — not that I think it will do any good.' That afternoon they had a swim at Gezira then at 1700hr went out to 239 Wing, but no flying was possible because of dust storms.

On the 25th (a Saturday) Marting got up at six o'clock and did an hour's flying in a Kittyhawk; then he went into Cairo again and stayed at Wellington House overnight. On the Sunday he did not fly — there were no operations 'owing to severe dust storms', the No 239 Wing ORB recorded — and on the Monday he was involved in a belly-landing incident:

> Wally Tribken and I were up at 0600hr and were to go up for dog fighting. They gave me the wrong 'plane — one that didn't belong to this Wing and was not serviceable. We had our dog fight and then went down for some shadow shooting. I stooged around as target for half an hour while Wally emptied his guns. When it was my turn, I found I couldn't cock my guns. They work on the same system as the wheels and flaps[4] and I couldn't get them down either. Came back to the airfield and circled, waggling my wings until they got out the ambulance and fire tenders and then did a belly landing. It did very little damage to the aircraft and none to me: it wasn't bad at all — just a sudden stop.

Tuesday, 28 July, turned out to be a key day in the RAF careers of the three Americans — though at the start it seemed little different from any of the others. Marting did an hour's flying after breakfast, then in the afternoon went in to Cairo for a swim. But their postings had come through:

> Found out that I'm going to No 450 Sqn, which is Australian. It's supposed to be the best in this Wing, which includes No 3 (Aussie), No 112 (mixed), No 250 (mixed) and 450. Miluck and Tribken are going to 250.

So their Desert Air Force futures were settled.

But until they actually got to their squadrons, and with the general military situation a static one — the Battle of Alam Halfa, when the Afrika Korps attempted to break out and open up the road to Alexandria, was still a month away — life went on much as before: a mix of practice-flying and recreational visits to Cairo, a spartan desert life and the fleshpots of the Delta.

Thus on 29–30 July, Marting recorded that he was up at 0500hr and 'got everyone else up who was supposed to fly', then 'had 40 minutes practice strafing' — instead of the shadow firing (that is, aiming at the shadow of another Kittyhawk flying low over the desert) he was supposed to do. By midday he was in Cairo, went swimming at Gezira in the afternoon and up on the roof of the Continental Hotel for drinks in the evening.

Staying at Wellington House, his night's rest was disturbed by an air raid at three o'clock in the morning: 'three Huns dropped bombs on the aerodrome at the edge of town and started some large fires. None fell on the city.'

By midday on the 30th he was back at LG91, where he 'slept most of the afternoon', and in the evening 'there was too much dust storm to fly'.

It was on 31 July that the Americans went to their squadrons, but at the beginning of the day a bizarre incident occurred, which Marting recorded in his diary:

> Woke up early this morning and as I walked from my tent to answer Nature's call, I saw one of our aircraft catch on fire in the air. He went down behind the hills in flames so I rushed down and got a truck and picked up the CFI, Bill Carsons[5], and we went over to the wreck. The pilot [had] got out all right, with only two small cuts on his face. His aircraft burned up.

Before the move he did half an hour's flying, 'but the kite was no good so quit', then he packed up his kit and got ready to leave. 'Miluck flew up to the squadron and Tribken and I came by truck. We are all in the same Wing and on the same landing ground[6], but they are 250 Sqn and I'm 450.

Tribken and I arrived here about 1800hr. Spent the evening in the Mess getting acquainted. The fellows are all OK and I think I'm going to like it.

On Saturday, 1 August 1942, the Americans' first day on their Desert Air Force squadrons, No 450 'went on two bombing shows' in the morning, but Marting 'didn't get to go'. He flew for half an hour in the afternoon on an air test — the first time he'd 'taken off and landed with a bomb on — a 500-pounder'[7] — and summed up his new situation:

The food we get here is much better than it has been out here yet. We also have plenty of water. Half a dozen of us went up the road for a shower this evening.
My situation is rather peculiar now. I'm an American serving in the RCAF attached to the RAF but in a RAAF squadron.

At this time No 239 Wing and its squadrons were given a rest from operations. Its ORB recorded on 2 August:

A signal was received from AAHQ (Advanced Air Headquarters) (Western Desert) releasing the Wing and squadrons from operations for a rest and training period, the intention being to grant all personnel seven days' leave, followed by ten days' intensive training to build up the squadrons for further intensive operations.

That morning, however, the squadrons had operated and Marting had 'got one in' before the stand-down. As he described it:

Had my first taste of desert operations today. Nine of this squadron and eight of No 250 took off from here about 1030hr and landed for refuelling at LG172.[8] We left there at noon, eleven carrying bombs, most of which were 500-pounders. We were top cover to 250 Sqn. After 45 minutes we arrived at our target, which was a concentration of tanks and trucks in a wadi near Qattara spring, about 100 miles in German territory.

Dropped our bombs and then came back twice to strike. I could not see my own 500-pounder hit but it was well within the target area. Strafed three trucks and a pill-box.
We left the target with a petrol dump burning and two trucks going up in flames and reckon all of the other trucks were well damaged. Two of our squadron were hit, one in the tail — which exploded an oxygen bottle and cut his rudder controls, the other in the radiator. We all got back OK. 250 Sqn lost one pilot, who had to force-land back there somewhere but may be all right. Our leader, Squadron Leader Haysom[9], had a shot through his oil tank but managed to get home. He was covered with oil from head to foot. The whole show took 2 hr 55 min.

Both squadron ORBs carried detailed descriptions of this operation. No 250's recorded that

Seven aircraft with Sqn Ldr Haysom as leader made a longer trip than usual to bomb an enemy land recce unit at Qattara Afrem on the edge of the Depression[10] about 70 miles due south of Mersa Matruh. Bombing was successful, five 500s and three 250s falling well among 25MT, one armoured car and two tents. One fire seen. Then our pilots strafed three times. Flt Lt Hancock hit the armoured car, Plt Off Collier one truck (possibly another also) and two tents or huts, WO Edwards saw bullets go into the side of a W/T vehicle with mast, Fg Off Taylor damaged one truck which he attacked twice and Plt Off Russel hit two MT while Plt Off Whiteside definitely damaged three more. Aircraft left LG91 at 0945hr, refuelling at LG172, which they left at 1220hr, returning direct to LG91 and landing at 1415hr. Leave begins tomorrow and eight pilots fly to Lydda.[11]

Miluck and Tribken were not involved: on the 1st the ORB had noted:

Fg Off Miluck and Plt Off Tribken, recent arrivals, did practice flying in the afternoon (no dust storms for a wonder).

No 450 Sqn, recording for the 2nd 'the longest operation yet made by this squadron ... when aircraft bombed Hisy Tartura about 72 miles due south of Mersa Matruh', recorded tersely:

Nine aircraft airborne 1013hr to LG172 for refuelling at 1033hr. Took off ... at 1215hr .... Route out direct to target ... at 7,000ft. Bottom cover, bombed and strafed. One aircraft in top cover then bombed from 300ft down on a concentration of 12 MET including two tanks and armoured vehicles stationary, not very well dispersed.... Bombing was good: bombs fell within ten yards of three vehicles, one of which was a tank or armoured car. Another bomb burst between two vehicles 40 yards apart. The strafing was particularly good with the following results: Sqn Ldr Ferguson[12], one truck destroyed; Plt Off Schaaf, one petrol dump (flamer); Flt Sgt McBurnie, four trucks damaged; Flt Sgt Law, one large truck (flamer); Fg Off Marting, three trucks damaged and MT post; Sgt Davidson, one truck destroyed, Flt Sgt Dyson, one tank slightly damaged.

So Hal Marting had his Western Desert baptism of fire, just before the stand-down:

'Our Wing is released for seven days' leave and two weeks' practice-flying. Am going back to Cairo for my week'[13], he wrote on the 2nd. But it was a leave which wasn't going to work out as he planned.

On Monday, 3 August, he wrote:

> Flew a 'plane back to 239 Base and came into Cairo last evening. Am staying at Wellington House again. Have a headache so am not going out tonight.

That headache was the beginning of something much worse. It was still with him the following morning so he stayed in bed:

> Have been feeling worse and think I have some fever. Had a friend call a doctor this afternoon and he sent me to hospital right away. I have either sand-fly-fever or malaria. Am in the RAF Hospital. It looks as if my leave is wrecked.

Wednesday, 5 August, was the turning-point in his illness. That morning he felt 'somewhat worse' but by the evening 'much better'. He had not had anything to eat for a couple of days ('feed a cold, starve a fever' the old maxim used to say) but on this day was given some Oxo meat extract to drink, which made him feel better.

His improvement continued: on the Thursday he 'felt somewhat better', though he still had a headache, but he felt hungry and his fever was 'just about gone'. Next day he recorded that he had 'not been feeling too bad' and that he had 'started eating full rations'. On the Saturday he was 'feeling very well' — the only signs of illness were 'slight weakness when walking around'. His appetite had come back and he ate a large breakfast; the doctor told him he could get up and that he could leave the hospital on the following day. That evening his friends found him: 'Miluck and Tribken came out to see me .... They've been up to Palestine for two days.'

But on Sunday, 9 August, when he found his release paper from the hospital waiting for him after breakfast, he was still 'pretty weak' so was 'just sitting around', and he was given an additional four days' leave in which to recover his strength.

Hal Marting spent this leave quietly, and even when he got back to the squadron, found himself comparatively inactive, which bored his impatient spirit — impatient, that is, to get back into operations.

On Monday, 10 August, he did some shopping in Cairo but was 'still a bit weak' so 'taking it easy for a few days yet. Just sat around and read ... and this evening ... didn't even go out.'

Next day he had tea with Lt Jimmy Weir, Royal Navy, whom he had met in Durban. 'He is second in command of a motor gun boat ... used against subs. It's just finished and he's very proud of it. He showed me each of its 110ft and I enjoyed it very much.'

That evening he 'ran into Bob Mannix[14] and we and Sqn Ldr Pegge, his CO,[15] went to the Metropole Night Club.'

Clearly Marting was anxious to get back into action. On the 12th he

> got up early ... and went back to camp. My leave isn't up for two more days so I think I'll go to Alexandria in the morning. There were several letters for me. The oldest was dated 22 January and there was one of 19 February. One [sent] in April and one from Grace[16] in May. Bob Ward[17] had written to me in England just a few days before I sailed: it is a pity he couldn't have written sooner.

He went off to Alexandria — 'cleaner than Cairo but ... still very dirty and the same stench prevails' — on the 13th, getting a lift in one of the squadron trucks and staying at the Windsor Palace Hotel, which 'wasn't too bad' and getting 'half tight' that evening with two Aussies he'd met during the afternoon.

But he wanted to get back to the squadron so the following morning hitched a ride back to LG91 (which was in fact much nearer to Alexandria than to Cairo), but before leaving 'bought purses for Fran and Marilyn[18], almost alike but one half as big as the other'. Mindful of the long-delayed mail he had just received he noted: 'if it takes as long as they say to reach the States, they should arrive just before Christmas'. That evening he went over to 250's Mess to 'see Miluck and Tribken — had a few beers with them'.

On Saturday, 15 August, Marting was back on flying — 45 minutes spent firing at the shadow of another aircraft as it flew over the desert: 'Almost as good practice', he commented, 'as shooting at an aircraft itself'. That afternoon, Ed Miluck came over to 450 Sqn and they 'went up the road ten miles for a shower', then Miluck stayed for dinner. Marting had an early night so as to be up the next morning for some more shadow firing.

At this time the No 239 Wing squadrons were still on an operational stand-down. Marting did an hour's shadow firing on the 16th; later that day, he noted, 'Miluck, Sly, Upward[19] and I went over to see Bob Mannix tonight and got a little tight.'

There was 'nothing doing' on the Monday, 17 August: 'just sat around playing the victrola[20] in the Mess'. Next morning he 'got a lift back to base in a Lysander'[21] then hitch-hiked into Cairo where he booked in at Wellington House.

On the 19th he 'rode out to base with our Wing Commander (Wing Commander G.D.L. Haysom) and flew back here in a Kitty for 112 Sqn.[22] Nothing doing today but our training period is over so we may expect operations from tomorrow on.'

He was right, because the next morning the squadron sent six aircraft to escort a Boston in which the AOC-in-C (Air Marshal Sir Arthur Tedder) was flying; but Marting 'didn't get on that show' — there was 'nothing to do all day again.' He was clearly fed up and on the 21st wrote:

No flying for me again today although the squadron went on a show this morning[23]. I expect I'll be on tomorrow. This inactivity is getting very boring. The war seems to be getting worse every day[24] and here I sit doing nothing! I'll be glad when I'm no longer under British command: they seem to be all in a muddle and none of the brass hats want to take any responsibility on their own.

We had an air raid tonight but there were no bombs dropped on this 'drome. Several were only two or three miles away and the Huns were flying directly over us.

Next day he was back on operations:

Went on an armed recce this morning for 1 hr 15 min but saw no enemy aircraft and no good target for my bomb so didn't drop it. The flak was very heavy and very accurate — I felt that I could reach out and touch a few bursts. One of the fellows in No 3 Sqn was hit and had to force-land but he was over our lines and OK.

On Sunday 23 August, No 450 Sqn 'did two shows' but Marting wasn't involved; but on the Monday he

was on another armed recce this morning for an hour and a half. Down in the southern sector of the Hun lines we passed over enormous concentrations of Panzer troops which threw up plenty of accurate flak. We dive-bombed them and my 250-pounder hit 30 or 40 yards from a large tent and truck. It was a 'stick' bomb so I imagine it did some damage. We all came back OK.

We had a party tonight for an entertainment group from South Africa. I was celebrating my 100th hour of operations[25] and got tight.

Dust storms were a problem for the Desert Air Force squadrons. On the 25th, after nine aircraft of 450 Sqn had done an armed recce over the forward area in the early morning, experienced intense light ack-ack over the target area but seen no enemy aircraft, it moved its Kittyhawks

during the afternoon to a landing-ground three or four miles
north of LG91 and at 1755hr six of them took off on another
armed recce — but 'the dust was so bad at the front we
couldn't even see the ground and it extended up to
8,000–9,000ft. We turned around and came back.'

There was no flying for Marting on the 26th, though six of
450's aircraft did an armed recce, 'so nothing to do but read
and sleep all day. Went for a shower this afternoon and over
to see Miluck and Tribken tonight. Came back early. Jerry
bombed a few miles from here tonight but didn't bother us.'

The same pattern was repeated, as far as Marting was
concerned, on the next two days: while 450 'did a bombing
show' on the 27th he was not involved; and on the 28th 'none
of us flew all day' but he was on 'readiness': 'Miluck and
Tribken came over with Sqn Ldr Devenish whom we knew at
Padgate.[26] We had a few beers. Jerry started a raid at about
2300hr and was bombing a 'drome down the road from here.
Nothing fell on us.' In the small hours of the next morning —
about 0430hr — they had another raid: 'bombs were dropped
all around us but not on us. One of the attackers was shot
down in flames by either a night fighter or ack-ack.' This
increased enemy activity was the prelude to the battle of
Alam Halfa — the attempted break-out by the Afrika Korps
— which began at the end of August.

On the 29th the Kittyhawk squadrons were in action again,
and Marting vividly described their operation:

> Was up at 0600hr this morning and four of us went on a
> bombing show with eight of No 3 (RAAF) Sqn. Our target
> was behind Jerry's lines in about the middle of the front.
> Shillabeer[27] was leading our four and I was leading the
> second section: we were top cover. Three 109s were over
> us as we reached the target and we stayed up until the
> other eight had bombed. Four of 3 Sqn were supposed to
> cover us, so we went down, but Shillabeer was attacked
> and shot down when he pulled out of the dive. My No 2
> and I joined the other fellows of 3 Sqn and climbed up as
> top cover; in the meantime the rest of the gaggle reversed

its turn and we became separated from them. Three 109s attacked us twice and were driven off as we turned into them. We went into a circle and after about ten minutes when we straightened out my No 2, Sgt Marble (RCAF), overshot me and was shot down by one of the Huns. I pulled up and squirted at this one but he was out of range. The remaining three of us started for home and the other section's No 2 was attacked, but I turned over them and into the Hun and gave him a squirt which drove him off. We then went down below cloud and scooted for home.

Went swimming at the beach this afternoon.

This casual remark highlights the fact that, at this static stage of the desert war, fighter pilots of the Desert Air Force — all extremely fit young men in the dry, warm Egyptian environment — might be swimming or sunbathing in the Alexandria area, a haunt of pre-war tourists, then only a few hours later, be involved in life-or-death combat above the battle lines around El Alamein, only 60 miles to the west.

On the following day (Sunday, 30 August) he recorded:

Nothing doing for me today. The squadron went on a fighter sweep and mixed it up with some 109s but knocked down none and lost none. We are supposed to be through with dive-bombing for a while.

In the early hours of Monday morning, 31 August, they were bombed — 'the Huns came very low and I saw one of them in the moonlight' — then later that day No 450 Sqn went on an operation:

We were close escort to ten Bostons and two B-25s[28] this morning but nothing happened. They bombed a concentration of motor vehicles and the bombing was very good.

Marting, Miluck and Tribken were still hankering after joining the USAAF, and that evening Marting set off for Cairo to visit the US Legation again and go for a medical examination.

He had left it late, starting at 1800hr, so only got as far as the Halfway House on the Alexandria–Cairo road and stayed the night there. The following day (1 September) he got in to Cairo at about eleven o'clock and met Miluck and Tribken at the US Legation, where 'they arranged for us to take the physical examination at the Army bomber station at Deversoir' — an airfield at the northern end of the Great Bitter Lake, near Ismailia — 'so we're going down there in the morning'.

They hitch-hiked there on the morning of the 2nd, arriving at about noon, and Marting set down a blow-by-blow account of their medical check-up in his diary:

> Our exam started at 3 pm so we had to finish the eye tests tonight because they had no dark room to work in. I'm amazed at my own condition. I passed the tests easily and the eye tests were conducted with very poor lighting conditions. My blood pressure, which was on the high limit when I enlisted two years ago, is now below normal for my age and is lower than Tribken's — who is just 24! In the Snyder test[29], which is most important, I had a rating of +14 — the limits are +8 and +18 (which is perfect). Miluck was +17 and Tribken +12. It makes me feel quite good to have passed a physical examination easily at the age of 31+ which I failed 13 years ago![30]
>
> The US bombers from here (B-25s — 81st Sqn., 12th Bombardment Group)[31] attacked airfields between El Daba and Fuka tonight and all got back unscathed.

On 3 September Marting, Miluck and Tribken 'hitched' a flight back to Cairo:

> Said goodbye to the American fellows this morning and they gave us a lift back here in one of their bombers. They were very nice to us and we enjoyed our visit.

That afternoon they took their papers to the US Legation, 'did a little shopping for some of the fellows and also bought three new swing records for the squadron Mess'. They had lunch at the New Zealand Club and 'stayed in that evening'.

Next morning they went to the US Legation again to take a letter from the Canadian Liaison Officer, then hitch-hiked out to LG91, getting there about 1400hr. Marting found letters awaiting him from 'Fran, Dad and Lennie'[32], and answered two of them that evening. He noted in his diary: 'They have given me my own 'plane now — OK-A'. He flew this aircraft for the first time on the following day and reported enthusiastically: 'it certainly is lovely. Only about four hours on it altogether.[33] It's faster than most of them and flies very nicely.'

On the afternoon of the 5th he was involved in a 'show' from LG175 (three miles east of the Cairo–Alexandria desert road and three miles north by west of end of Nubariya Canal, at position 3055N 2955E) — 'a scramble to intercept enemy 'planes in the Burg-el-Arab area' (just north of the railway line from Alexandria to El Alamein). 'They were higher than us and according to reports out-numbered us about three to one, so we were glad they didn't come down. We were top cover and in a ticklish spot'.[34]

Next morning (a Sunday) he was on 'readiness' and 'placed as top cover for my squadron, which was to be top cover for No 3 Sqn, escorting bombers to El Daba aerodromes' (about 30 miles west of El Alamein). 'That is one hot spot', he added; he was 'surprised to be given that responsibility on that show' — but 'for some reason it was cancelled'; all he did was a 45-minute air test in the afternoon.

On the 7th, however, it all really happened. No 450 Sqn were on 'readiness' at 1000hr with No 3 Sqn: Marting was 'placed as Yellow 1, Flt Lt Parker leading our ten aircraft and No 3 Sqn as top cover. Both squadrons were scrambled and Parker had to turn back, leaving me leading the whole business' — the first time he had 'ever led the whole show. We were vectored on to a big party of Huns at 15,000ft — there were 20+ of them to our 16. We didn't make contact, fortunately, and came on home. I was glad of that, but I did all right and was only a little nervous.'

That afternoon he did an hour's shadow firing — his partner was Plt Off Sly again — and in the evening 'took a truck down to LG99 (15 miles southeast of Amiriya) and brought back eight of the US Army from there. They had dinner with us and we had a very good party. They are having trouble getting their food and were amazed to see our steak, peas, onions and potatoes for dinner and would hardly believe this wasn't out of the ordinary'.

Marting had a change of scene on the 8th when he 'got the Wing's Lysander[35] and flew Flt Lt Matthews down to base[36] and then went on to Deversoir to get two larynx microphones from the US Army.[37] Got back about 1500hr, the trip taking three hours' flying time. It was the first time I've ever flown a 'Lizzie' — don't care much for them.' In the evening Bob Mannix came over and they went to 250 Sqn 'to have dinner and several drinks with Tribken and Miluck.'

For the next two days there was no action: on the 9th No 450 Sqn were on 'readiness' from 1130hr; they took their aircraft over to LG175 to operate from there but 'didn't do anything' and brought them back at 1600hr. Marting got his throat mike 'all rigged up' and it was 'much better than the old ones'. He went to bed early, in preparation for early 'readiness' the next day, but on the 10th there was a 'terrific dust storm', so 'nothing doing at all'.

Three of No 239 Wing squadrons — Nos 3, 112 and 450 — twenty aircraft in all — were involved in a fighter sweep on the 11th, Marting leading 450's top four; but though they were out for more than an hour, they saw nothing.

He 'missed a good show' on the 12th, when his squadron 'ran into a Stuka party':[38] Flt Lt Williams got one Stuka destroyed and confirmed and one 109 probable. Sgt Taylor got one 109 damaged and Sgt Oakley one 109 destroyed confirmed and one probable. All that without loss or even a bullet hole! There were also two other confirmed victories in other squadrons in this Wing and several damaged and probables'. Marting 'didn't get to fly' and that afternoon went into Alexandria with Flt Lt Parker, Plt Off Law and Sgt Phelps; they played golf at the Sporting Club, and while he 'hit the ball fairly well the scoring was poor'. As a connoisseur, he noted that 'the course was well ... kept but not as sporty as Cairo's'.

On Sunday, 13 September, he was in action again:

> was Green 1 in top cover and we were scrambled out over the front to intercept the enemy. We ran into them all right but they stayed up above us, only one coming down to make any attempt to attack. He went right back up so none of us had a squirt.

Marting had another Cairo trip in the Lysander on the 14th, taking Flt Sgts Dyson and McBurnie with him.[39] Had lunch at the New Zealand Club and then came back here in the afternoon. Bought two rolls of movie film to get some pictures to take back. Am borrowing Flt Sgt Sheppard's camera.'

That day — lunch and shopping in Cairo — and the next, when Marting was involved in a desperate combat, illustrate two aspects of the desert air war at that time: the proximity of the 'fleshpots' of Cairo and Alexandria while the 8th Army was at El Alamein, and the 'war of attrition' which was the lot of the fighter pilots while there was a military stalemate on the ground.

On the 15th Marting started using his movie film: he got some pictures taken of himself 'getting into my Kitty, and some of all the fellows'. Then suddenly the scene changed when he went on readiness at 1700hr and again was Green 1 on top cover:

> We were scrambled with No 3 Sqn and over the central front we ran into 20+ 109s. There were eighteen of us and they came down in one big bunch to attack. We were at 12,000ft and the Huns at about 17–18,000ft. During the ensuing dog-fight we were joined by 250 and 112 Sqns so there were at least 50 aircraft involved. They came at us

out of the sun and in a couple of seconds there was no formation left — just one big mass milling around the sky. I saw a 109 on the tail of a Kitty and went for him. He was turning away from me and when I opened fire, my shots hit him in the belly. I was forced to break off then as another was attacking me head on. Had a couple more long-range shots which missed; then I saw a Kitty diving in front of me which turned out to be Sgt O'Neil. My first squirt made the 109 pull up, and I followed, firing all the time in quick bursts. When he reached the top of his climb he rolled on his back, and as he rolled, my shots hit the 109's belly from about 100 yards. He fell on his back for a second and then nosed down — with me right after him. As he dived he rolled back right side up. I followed him down to 4,000ft and saw him go straight into the ground and explode in a great big sheet of flame. There were three other 'planes burning on the ground already. I climbed back up to the scrap and saw two parachutes coming down right in the middle of it and a third on the ground. The Jerries decided about then that they'd had enough and left. Two aircraft collided in the melée, but I didn't see it happen. Sgt Ewing is missing from our squadron and two of our 'planes were damaged. No 3 Sqn lost two fellows but I haven't heard the score of the whole thing yet.

On the 16th, when he 'didn't get to fly ... so there was nothing to do but take some more movies and read most of the day', he learned the score: 'Found out that there are six missing from yesterday's show. The army at the front reported 13 aircraft coming down, so that puts us ahead, seven to six. There are two missing from 250 Sqn and one from 112'.[40]

Marting had a 'prang' on take-off from LG91 on the 17th. He'd been on early morning readiness but 'there was nothing doing' and at 1330hr they were 'told to fly over to LG175 on account of dust here. Taking off I hit a bad bump ... which bounced me into the air and skidded me sideways into Sgt

MacFarlane's slipstream, which lifted my wing and turned me to the right. I hit with quite a jolt, tearing off both wheels and breaking the wings. Luckily one of the fellows behind me didn't take off because of engine trouble or he would have run right into me. The pranged aircraft was OK-V (EV169), the CO's [Sqn Ldr A.D. Ferguson] and not mine, OK-A.'

For the next two weeks there was 'nothing doing' operationally, but on the 18th Marting made a new acquaintance — an Me 109 — and on the 23rd met an old friend from 71 Sqn days, Plt Off Leo Nomis.[41]

Clearly still thinking he might be off to join the USAAF at any time — 'wasn't on today but there was nothing doing anyway. I think we are conserving our aircraft for a big push which may start most any time now — I hope before I leave the squadron' — he 'went over to take a look at a 109 which they have here on the 'drome now. It had been shot down with very little damage and is now in flying condition. I hope to fly it soon: it's the most compact machine I've ever seen and is so small it looks like a toy. It's beautifully built and the only thing I don't like about it is the poor visibility from the cockpit'. He wanted to film it: 'started the third 50ft reel of movies today and am going to try to get some of the 109 in the air'.

After another day's inactivity on the 20th and readiness on the 21st, but 'nothing doing', he 'went to see the Wing Commander (Wg Cdr Haysom) after lunch and got 48 hours' leave to go to Cairo. Flew up this afternoon in a Bombay'.[42]

Marting could not get in at his usual haunt, Wellington House, so stayed in a small pension (boarding-house) on the Monday night and next morning went to the US Legation. There they told him that it could be 'only a matter of days' before they heard from Washington about his transfer to the USAAF. In the afternoon he went to the Gezira Club for a swim and in the evening to the 'Dug Out' bar in the Metropole Hotel, for a drink.[43]

When the next morning (Wednesday 23 September) he went to the New Zealand Club for breakfast he got a big surprise. 'Ran into Plt Off Nomis who was in 71 Sqn with us.

He has been to Malta and was sent here for transfer to the US Army. He got the French *Croix de Guerre* in Malta for something the RAF tried to court martial him for! He took a Spit off at night without permission, flew to Sicily and shot down a Heinkel III, wrecked a train, shot up some houses and came back all right.'[44] Marting decided to take Nomis back with him to 450 Sqn for a few days' visit.

On the morning of the 24th they met at Wellington House and hitch-hiked out to LG91, arriving at about 1500hr. 'Tribken and Miluck came over to our Mess tonight and got the surprise of their lives,' Marting recorded in his diary, adding the sad note: 'News from 71 Sqn isn't so good. Eight or ten have been killed since we left.'[45]

As there was nothing doing operationally next day, Marting borrowed a jeep and took Nomis over to look at the Me109, then to LG174 (three miles due east of LG91) where USAAF squadrons were located.

On the morning of Saturday, 26 September, Marting was on readiness but 'did nothing' — which made me sore because I was leading the Wing and wanted a chance at it.' He added: 'We are getting new aircraft — Kittyhawk IIIs. These have the 1370 hp Allisons so should be better. Their US designation is P-40K. Went down the road about six miles to help collect them and flew one back. It seemed fine and faster.' That evening, he noted, 'had six of the pilots from the USAAF Pursuit Squadron 66 over for dinner. They were nice fellows and we enjoyed having them.'[46]

Marting flew Leo Nomis back to Cairo on Sunday, 27 September, returning to LG91 by 1300hr. In the afternoon he took one of the new Kittyhawk IIIs up for a test and reported that it was 'better than the old ones', adding: 'I hate to give up my old OK-A but I get one of the new kites tomorrow and am going to make it OK-A too'.

Next morning he went out to his new aircraft and 'looked on while they harmonized the guns and gun-sight and prepared everything for operations. It's brand new — has only four or five hours on it — and the groundcrew and I are very proud of it. Sgt MacFarlane is sharing it with me and he

tested it and found everything perfect.' That morning
Marting flew for an hour (though not in 'A', which wasn't
ready in time) 'practising battle formations with nine others.
The squadron was on readiness this afternoon and four of the
US pilots from 64 Sqn were on with them. They are to fly
with us for a while to get some experience'.

There was no action on the last two days of September. On
the 29th Marting 'went up on a practice formation' in the
afternoon and after about 40 minutes Plt Off Schaaf and
myself broke off, ostensibly to have a practice dog-fight. We
had arranged beforehand that we were going over the front
to look for trouble. Went over at 16,000ft but didn't see a
thing'. After they got back to LG91 they were on readiness
but 'didn't get off the ground'. That evening half a dozen of
the pilots paid a return visit to the USAAF 66 Pursuit
Squadron: 'had quite a lot of beer and a nice time'.

Next day there was 'nothing doing'; in the afternoon
Marting did an hour's 'practice flip'.

There was action for part of the Wing, however, on 1
October: No 450 was on readiness in the morning 'but nothing
came up' and 'it didn't get off the ground'; it was scrambled in
the afternoon but 'didn't find anything'. Then, 'right after they
took off, 250 and 112 were scrambled and ran into a Stuka
party and knocked down two without loss to themselves.'

Edward Miluck vividly described this action in his own
diary, which began at that date:

> 'Stukas at nine o'clock', the radio spluttered, and I
> began to sweat. They were coming straight out of the
> west — 18 of them, with a dazzling sunset behind them.
> Our leader was so excited none of us could understand
> his squeaking, but we climbed instinctively to get into
> position for attack. The most amazing thing was the
> ugliness of the Stukas, with their wheels hanging down
> — big clumsy birds of prey, heavy with unlaid eggs.[47]

> 'Messerschmitts coming down!' The sweat really began
> to pour: it looked like a warm and sticky 'do'. Half our

flight started for the 20 Messerschmitts, and soon it was a shambles up there and a massacre down below — so many damned 'planes buzzing about I kept wishing my 50mm calibres were shotguns. The Stukas began jettisoning their bombs and that was a delightful sight — they were directly over their own lines. I think I damaged a 109 as he overshot me and climbed past my nose, and I also managed to make a head-on attack into a Stuka. The bullets sparked against its engine, but I had to turn away before I saw what happened, as tracers were streaking past my wings from behind. Returning to the shambles, I overtook a Stuka diving for the ground and helped him on his way with all I had left. It must have been enough — he hit with a hell of a thump. When I looked around again, five or six Jerries were burning in the air and the rest were limping off. The score: six Stukas destroyed, six probably destroyed, many more aircraft damaged. We had forced them to bomb their own troops. No 250's twelve aircraft were by some miracle intact, without a single bullet hole in their fuselages. Two Me109s overtook me on the way home and their strange behaviour puzzled me: passing over 500ft above me, the leader did a half roll and took a good look before rolling out and stooging on. The second did exactly the same thing. As I was out of ammunition I could only stick the nose down and weave like hell, keeping them always in sight in case they decided to play, but they ignored me and climbed back toward their own lines.

For No 450 Sqn there was a surprise order that day: 'We were told to pack up this afternoon, that the squadron was moving back to LG222 (ten miles SSW of the Giza Pyramids, on the east side of the Cairo-Fayoum road) for the defence of Cairo because of some daylight raids they've been having. We're pretty mad about it. Got everything packed and all the tents down this evening so we sleep out tonight'.

Marting was to pay a penalty for sleeping out that night, and for his squadron there was some confusion about its orders. The next day (Friday, 2 October) started well: 'Woke up early this morning and had a fine breakfast of eggs and bacon right out in the open. The convoy trucks pulled out about eight and the aircraft left right after. We'd been told to go to LG222 and went, only to find that they'd made a mistake and we have to come over to LG224 — 26 kilometres from Cairo. Worked all afternoon getting the tents up and baggage unpacked. Had a nice cool sponge bath before dinner. Am going to bed early'.

On the following day he went into Cairo early in the morning to chase up his transfer to the USAAF. There was 'no news' at the American Legation but he got them to send off a 'chaser' cable; then he had lunch at the New Zealand Club and got back to LG224 (Cairo West) late in the afternoon, when he experienced the first sign of trouble: 'I seem to have caught a cold the night before last when we slept out. I have a very sore throat so I don't think I'll fly for a few days'. That evening a desert phenomenon occurred: 'A very peculiar dust storm blew up just at sunset. An enormous cloud 20 or 30 miles long and 3,000–4,000ft high just rolled across the desert. It was quite clear before and after and it lasted only an hour.'

Marting did nothing on 4 October — he was not flying on account of his sore throat, so 'just sat around all day and read' — but Miluck was operational that evening. He 'sunbathed most of the day, also scrounged enough water for a bath in a canvas basin', then

> was lucky enough to get in on another dusk show, this time dive-bombing some motor transport. Bags of ack-ack over the target, too damned close for comfort. In fact I definitely heard six bursts explode nearby and was tossed on my back twice. Nice, oily, black puffs with huge orange balls of flame in their centers — quite harmless-looking. After we'd released our bombs, three 109s attacked, but they climbed straight up as we turned into them. Must have been new pilots, for they exposed

their grey bellies and treated us to an excellent close-up of the black-and-white crosses on their wings. Too bad they were moving so fast; a nice burst into one of those smooth bellies would have meant curtains for some Jerry.

While Miluck was still in action at LG91 (or potentially so: 'No longer a precipital virgin, by God!' he recorded sardonically on the 5th. 'It rained and hailed this afternoon for one minute and forty-six seconds. The wind blew and the bull flew.[48] Lovely moonlight. Very romantic') Marting was, like the mighty Achilles at Troy, sulking in his tent at LG224 — until he could stand it no longer and went in to Cairo. 'Sitting around at the camp is too much for my nerves', he noted. 'I got disgusted this morning so just packed a bag and came in. Don't know what they'll say about it and don't care much. Went down to the Metropolitan Hotel tonight and ran into Bob Mannix[49] so we got a little tight. No news at the US Legation yet'. He was clearly still hankering after his transfer to the USAAF, especially with 450's current lack of activity.

On the 6th, Marting went to the Gezira Club in the morning and played some golf; he also bought himself a book on chess which he read that afternoon and 'found very interesting', and he met a VIP: 'Lord Trenchard visited us here at Wellington House this afternoon. He is the founder of the RAF and is now Marshal of the Royal Air Force, the same rank as the King. Although nearly 80, he still pilots occasionally.'[50] That evening Marting stayed in and 'had a couple of games of chess'.

He played 18 holes of golf on the 7th with two 'pros' at the Gezira Club: 'had a good round which was only two over par and included three birdies'. But being AWOL (absent without official leave) was catching up on him: 'received a message at Wellington House that I must report back to the squadron first thing tomorrow'. That night LG91 was attacked — Miluck vividly described the scene in the early hours:

After admiring another brilliant moon and the tranquil peace of the desert, retired to bed at midnight. Then it began — that familiar drone of Jerry engines[51]; how well I remembered it from England. I hadn't bothered to dig a slit trench, so I decided to ignore them. Not so Wally. He started to dress and was already leaving the tent when it suddenly dawned on me that it was **our** airfield they were after. Stark naked, with only my tin helmet, I flew out of the tent at his heels. We'd reached the halfway mark to the nearest slit trench when down the bombs came and we fell flat on our faces. I noticed that my torch was still shining and tried to turn it off, but my fingers were too shaky. Wally kept yelling, 'put that goddam light out!' and finally I had to lie on top of it, feeling as if I were lying on a powerful searchlight with every damned Jerry in the sky watching me. There I was, with one hand trying to dig a hole in the sand and with the other holding a tin helmet over my backside. As the old song says:

> Look for me by moonlight;
> Watch for me by moonlight;
> I'll come to thee by moonlight,
> Though hell may bar the way.

Two of our aircraft were destroyed and three damaged: the bullets of one of them were still popping at breakfast-time when we went out to view the dozen-odd craters in the middle of the airfield.

On the 8th Marting received his come-uppance for his truancy: 'Got back to LG224 about ten. Got a little hell from the CO (Sqn Ldr A.D. Ferguson) but he rather sympathized with me and suggested I go talk to the AOC (Air Vice-Marshal Coningham).[52] I got as far as LG91 and our Wing Commander (Wg Cdr Haysom) who talked me out of seeing the AOC, so I got no satisfaction at all. Am staying overnight with 250 Sqn (Miluck and Tribken). They called here and told me not to go back in the morning as 450 is coming up here to operate tomorrow. Our information is that the Jerries are bogged down in mud and we're going to work over their aerodromes. Sounds good.'

Writing at midnight on the 9th, Miluck recalled that day's events:

> Due to recent heavy rains and the resulting sticky mud, Kesselring[53] got caught with all of his Me109s concentrated in a small area on several 'dromes. The entire RAF went into high gear at dawn and hasn't let up yet. Where the fighters and day medium bombers left off, the night bombers took over. Every field in the El Daba area[54] has been bombed, dive-bombed and strafed. On our first show we just bombed; on the other three we bombed and strafed. On the second, we were attacked by several 109s and I squirted at one for a hell of a long time. When the next one came by, I remembered to turn on my gun switch and did much better. Flt Sgt Rodney forgot to come back, and an Englishman 'bought it' this morning, making the score two to one, not in our favour. Wally (Tribken) tangled with a dozen Macchi 202s[55] and Me109s but escaped with four canon slugs in his cockpit and minor holes in fuselage and wing. When he crash-landed on the airfield the poor kite just sighed and collapsed. So did Wally.

Marting wasn't involved in the first of these sorties but in the second: '450 came up early this morning,' he wrote. 'I was up and waiting for them but damned if they would let me go on the first show — and, of course, that one that I missed turned out to be the only good one. Nos 3 and 450 followed the bombers and strafed the airfield at Daba after the bombs went down. They destroyed quite a number of 'planes on the ground. The escort shot down eight 109s without loss! 450 was the only one to lose a 'plane. Sgt Holloway is missing but it's believed he force-landed in the sea near the enemy coast. I was on the second show as close escort to 18 bombers which raided another airfield at El Daba. Saw seven 109s which were very shy. We got no flak either so that was no fun at all.'

On the 10th Marting was back at LG224 and Miluck had a very near miss:

> Very short of aircraft [he noted] as a result of yesterday. Only three of us, instead of the usual 'lonely six', formed top cover for two other Kittyhawk squadrons[56] dive-bombing some motor transport. Very boring, sitting up there on top and watching the others work. While I was admiring their efforts and enjoying the excellent view from 20,000ft, I forgot to keep the old eagle eye. So, of course, it happened: Heinrich, followed by Cousin Herman and Cousin Peter, proceeded to fill my kite full of .303in slugs. After a severe case of heart failure I managed by fiendish manoeuvring to snuggle into the middle of the bottom formation, cutting ahead of everyone except the leader — and I would have passed him if I could. Severe finger trouble on the part of yours truly, and I'm still scared and still shaking. What you see won't hurt you; it's what you don't see that clobbers you.

By contrast, Marting had an uneventful time:

> Was on readiness about six hours today but there were no scrambles. Had a flip in one plane to test the wireless with the controller at Heliopolis[57] but that only lasted 20 minutes because I couldn't get the wheels to go all the way up. Have spent quite some time reading my new book on chess and working out the problems. Am going to write a letter to Dad and then get to bed early.

The next day, a Sunday (11 October), he got airborne in the morning and went into Cairo in the evening: 'Had one hour', he noted, 'flying in practice dive-bombing with 20lb smoke bombs this morning. Wrote a letter to Marilyn then after lunch had another flip for 45 minutes testing a new aircraft we got this morning. Went into Cairo with some of the fellows tonight and had dinner at the New Zealand Club and a bath at Wellington House while the others went to the movies. They were late getting out and we didn't get home until nearly 3 am.'

In the afternoon of 12 October he did one and a half hours' practice flying, half of it leading a six-strong formation, the other half shadow-firing. 'My shooting has certainly improved', he noted; 'out of about ten shots at a shadow today, I only missed twice. Plt Off Winn, who was my No 2 today, took some pictures in the air which I hope come out good. Flt Lt Shepperd and Flt Lt Matthews showed several rolls of movies they took at Sidi Haneish, Bardia, Gambut and Halfaya Pass,[58] which were quite good. The CO has given me permission to take a trip in a Halifax soon: it should be interesting — they bomb Tobruk nearly every night'.[59]

That morning Miluck had been scrambled, on a patrol over the El Alamein line, 'but nothing to see except some pretty clouds. Flt Sgt Holmes force-landed, wheels up, with a frozen engine.[60] After six beers he was able to relax and tell us what happened'. Then there was this comment on living conditions in the Western Desert: 'Bloody flies! Not to mention the body lice, variously known as mobile dandruff or fuzz bunnies'.

But things were to change soon and in the next couple of days the AOC, Western Desert Air Force, Air Vice-Marshal Sir Arthur Coningham, visited the Kittyhawk squadrons to tell them what was in store.

On the 13th Marting had flown down to Fayid 'to see the new Marauders (B-26)[61] and to see if I couldn't get a ride on one of the Halifax bombers over Italy some night. Found out that it would take a lot of red tape so abandoned the idea'. That afternoon he was on readiness 'but nothing happened', and 450 was told that it was on the move: 'We were notified to pack up for the front again and we are all thankful. Am sleeping in the open tonight as our tent is already down.'

No 250 Sqn had had their briefing from the AOC that day. At first light, Miluck recorded, they

did a dawn show of 12 aircraft with the 66th Fighter Squadron, USAAF, on top, and a very pleasant 'op' it was. We dropped some lovely 500-pounders right in the middle of a cluster of motor transport, with the boys from home watching out for 109s. The AOC, AVM Coningham, had tea with us today and gave us a pep talk on the awaited push, which is scheduled for full moon time — about the 23rd or 24th[62]. He spoke of supplies, supplies and more supplies as the determining factor for victory, also mentioned that our El Daba show [on the 9th] pasted hell out of Jerry and destroyed numerous aircraft on the ground. Our job is just to shatter the *Luftwaffe* in the next ten days. The army will then push. Paddy Cairns[63], who has heard the same lecture before the last two pushes, seemed a bit pessimistic; but at least the talk created a new angle for conversation. The AOC seems to lack our deep respect for Jerry: he radiates confidence.

No 450 came up into the line the following day, 14 October, and had their briefing from the AOC in the afternoon. Heading his diary entry LG224/91/175, Marting recorded that he was

up before dawn and had breakfast at 0600hr. The convoy of trucks pulled out at about 0800hr and we took off about 0830hr. Had lunch with Ed and Wally at 250's Mess then flew on over to LG175 where we will operate from. The AOC called on us this afternoon to give us the information on the coming push which is about to start. According to AVM Coningham we're going to push the enemy right out of Africa. We are numerically superior by about four to one in troops and five to three in aircraft, so they think it will be a 'cinch' this time. This Wing and two others and 12 or 13 squadrons will be the main striking force in the air[64] and we are the ones chosen to go all the way as far as the push goes. I think the US Navy is going to have to wait for me.

Early that morning No 250 had been in action and later that day Miluck experienced the vicissitudes of desert life. First, 'another dawn bombing of El Daba, and another very pleasant "op". We began a gentle dive from 20,000ft, but by the time I pulled out at 6,000ft I was going straight down. Counted 11 hits and a lousy miss — probably mine. Watched the Me109s scramble, for a change, as we flew over and thumbed our noses at them on our way home'. Then at 1030hr the squadron was released for a parade to mark a visit by MRAF Lord Trenchard, whose '35-minute talk was humorous and enlightening', and in the afternoon Miluck 'retired to Alexandria for some good food and a shower with some real hot water'; but the day was to end disastrously: 'Returned at midnight in the damp cold, it having rained heavily, and found half the tents down due to the wind. Just a heap of mud-soaked canvas. A four-blanket night, and me sleeping outside because my tent was too wet to put up. Am getting a little dubious about Egyptian winters .... C'est la guerre. One might as well say, with Lin Yu Tang[65], "Nothing matters to a man who says that nothing matters" — but home was never like this!'

On the 15th Marting spent the morning rearranging his baggage — 'so that I can live with only one suitcase; that's all we'll be allowed on the push — one bag and a bedroll' and was on the first of two 'shows' in the afternoon, when 450 went alone — 'six with 500lb bombs and six as top cover: we bombed the railway station at Sidi El Rahman. My bomb made a direct hit on the rails about 50 yards east of the station. One other bomb hit the station itself and yet another hit directly in front of it, so the bombing was pretty good. We saw no enemy aircraft but the flak was fierce.'

450 had their visit from Lord Trenchard on the morning of the 16th at LG175: he gave them 'a very interesting talk for nearly an hour'; then at 1145hr Marting took off on an armed reconnaissance.

We went back of Jerry's lines around the south end and looked for an emergency airfield he's been using: we found possibly two. I dropped my 500lb bomb on a well-dug-in group of tents and motor vehicles and scored a very lucky hit. A few minutes later I strafed five trucks with two long bursts and saw hits on all of them. Eleven of us went out — six with bombs — and all returned though Sgt Fourneau had a flak shot through his wing. The flak was very accurate and intense. No scratches on lucky me.

Then the weather struck, as both diarists vividly recounted: on the 16th, Marting recorded, there was 'a terrible dust storm all the afternoon with a 30mph wind. Visibility was about 20ft. Tonight the wind is still howling and it's raining hard. Had to wade through mud to get to our tent tonight.'

On the 17th they recounted two different solutions to the weather problem. For Marting, a weekend in Cairo: 'The wind raged all night and there were intermittent showers. I got quite chilly. It continued all day and by 0900hr the water had dried and the dust was blowing again so badly there was no flying at all. Hitch-hiked into Cairo this afternoon. A truck is bringing in my baggage in the morning so I can store it at Cox and King's[66] with the rest. Bought myself a pair of pants and a shirt which I'm going to need. Am tired tonight and staying in.'

For Miluck and his fellow 250 Sqn pilots at LG91 it was a case of making the best of things:

A miserable morning, with an ever-increasing wind stirring the damp dust and black sand, and with clouds covering the horizon. Gulped down a gritty breakfast of beans, bacon, bread and jam, plus a cup of tepid coffee. A week ago I drank my first coffee; now I drink it regularly or go thirsty. What one won't do for Democracy!

"Ops" has released us for the day. It's raining sheets and buckets and the Mess tent leaks in a million places. It's soaking wet and so am I. The pilots are huddled in the dim, dry corners, smoking and drinking beer — the only liquid available. Thank God for the phonograph: at least Bing Crosby is still singing *I Can't get Indiana off my*

Mind — neither can I, Bing, neither can I. The new record *Concerto for Two* that I bought in Alexandria for the squadron is very popular, but the sand is beginning to ruin it already.

At six o'clock Wally and Troke[67] brought some beer and invited several squadrons over. We're seated in a big circle with the beer in the centre and a barrel for the empty cans. The barrel isn't the only thing that's full.

Marting's baggage arrived safely in Cairo at half-past one on the 18th (a Sunday) and he got it stored. As the truck wasn't going back to LG175 until the following day he decided to stay overnight and in the afternoon 'went around pricing movie cameras'. He had decided if possible to buy one 'to get some pictures of the coming push' — ordinary cameras were so hard to get in Egypt that movies were 'just about as cheap'. Leo Nomis was in town so that evening they went to The Dugout for a few drinks. He got his camera, a Kodak 8mm cine — having got up early on the Monday morning and 'between the bank and the paymaster raised £15', and used it to good effect on the way back to the desert that afternoon, taking 'nearly half a roll of film (20ft) of Cairo and the Pyramids'. Back at LG175 he found a letter from Bobby Locke ('still on an instructor's course in South Africa') waiting for him, and as he was 'on an early show in the morning' went to bed early.

Tuesday, 20 October, was an exciting day for Marting and Miluck: with only three days to go before the start of the El Alamein offensive, the Kittyhawk squadrons were escorting the light bombers in their attacks on Axis airfields, supplies and communications — in effect, a long-range artillery barrage to 'soften up' the enemy before the 8th Army went onto the offensive. Marting's aircraft was one of 12 of 450 Sqn which took off from LG175 at 0830hr as escort to twenty-four Baltimores and B-25s, attacking the Fuka landing grounds, providing top cover, while close and medium cover were provided by 66 Sqn (USAAF) and 3 Sqn. (RAAF) respectively.

The bombing was beautiful — the best I've ever seen [he recorded in his diary] and three large fires were burning on the 'drome as we left. On the way back we were attacked by six or seven 109s and Macchi 202s. The first one seen came up behind Plt Off Winn and I turned into him and fired from about 600 yards, closing down to 400 yards. My No 2, Prowse, saw my shots hit and the Macchi went into the ground about a mile behind. It was a lucky shot as three of my guns stopped and I only used a hundred rounds altogether. Flt Lt Clark damaged three 109s and was badly shot up himself. Winn had one or two holes in his tail and Gregory was badly shot up too. We had no losses and mine was the only confirmed victory.

Miluck was on a larger sortie, having tested his new aircraft earlier in the morning and been 'very pleased with the sensitive aileron controls'. 250 Sqn took off at 1130hr as close cover to twenty-four Baltimores and Mitchells again attacking Fuka airfield, LG17, about 20 miles west of Daba. 'Our flight was ahead and to one side of the bombers, thus unable to attack a 109 exchanging shots with a rear gunner. At one time top cover and medium cover were so far out of position that they were below the bombers; but 450 Sqn stayed on top and Marting destroyed a Macchi 202. Somewhere in the mix-up Flt Sgt A.E. Roberts, an American of 20 summers, got shot down'. In the aftermath of that day's battles Miluck wrote: 'Went over to 450 Sqn this afternoon to congratulate Marting and stayed for tea, but felt too tired to stay later. The strain is really wearing, though no one will admit it. Most of us are in bed these days by half-past seven'. But the strain continued, as the air offensive built up unremittingly towards the battle of El Alamein. The next day, Miluck recorded:

In the morning show we were close escort to 18 bombers. Due to low clouds they dived down from 5,000ft to bomb, then foolishly separated. The shambles was on: attacks from all sides by 109s and 202s. Falconer-Taylor was last seen dog-fighting with two 109s and someone said he was screaming for help.[68]

In our second show we were top cover escorting bombers to Fuka. Went as far as Daba, then broke away to dive-bomb and streak home. Of the six 109s that attacked, every one ignored the big show and attacked our squadron. Sgt R.C. Taylor was last seen flying towards a 109, both of them straight and level.

Marting had been on readiness from dawn on the 21st and was scrambled at about eight o'clock: 'We patrolled for half an hour but didn't see anything.' Then he 'led top cover of our squadron on a bomber escort at noon to Daba: 3 Sqn were top cover to us and they had some fun with twelve 109s. Too tired to get to the bombers but pulled off when we turned into them. I didn't get a shot at anything'. That afternoon he did an hour's flying 'to test the guns and long-range tank on my "A" — have been having too much gun trouble; had five stoppages again today'.

In the midst of these pre-El Alamein battles, Miluck commented on some of the squadron's supply difficulties, saying that messing was 'certainly the most important' of its many problems — especially in view of the impending advance, if the offensive was successful.

By chipping in about £2 each per month to supplement our airmen's rations, we manage a pretty good variety; but supplies will be uncertain when we start to move. As Messing Officer, Wally is arranging with 66 Sqn (USAAF) to exchange foodstuffs. They say the Wogs (Wily Oriental Gentlemen) barter eggs and other foods for tea, so he's collecting all he can and storing it for the big push. In the last one, the Wogs bartered eggs for tea leaves until the Aussies spoiled it by using the leaves first and drying them again in the sun.

On the 22nd neither Marting nor Miluck was operational. 'The squadron went on another bomber escort over Daba this morning', wrote Marting at LG175 of 450's activities, 'but I wasn't on. We lost two — Sgts Evans and Lindsey, two nice boys. Apparently the flak got them as there were no 109s near, and the fellows say it was the worst they'd ever seen. 3 Sqn also lost one, and two of the B-25s were lost.' During the morning he tested his guns in 'A' but there were still stoppages — 'so they've taken the guns out to work on them', and the aircraft was taken off operations. In the afternoon the squadron was 'supposed to go on a fighter sweep' but this was cancelled just as they were ready to take off. 450's new CO, Sqn Ldr J.E.A. Williams (Sqn Ldr Ferguson had handed over prior to going to HQ RAF ME), had told them that the "push" would start at 2200hr the following day. Marting, who was 'on again early in the morning — we're carrying bombs this time', commented in his diary: 'There will be no rest for us for some time now! This coming battle here is intended to be the turning-point of the war, so I'm proud to be in the main striking force'. But for Hal Marting, as we shall see, it was to be only a brief encounter with the enemy in the air — though not on the ground.

Miluck's day on the 22nd was also one of inactivity, as he sardonically recorded:

> Paddy Cairns and the CO (Sqn Ldr Judd) each destroyed a 109 on the first show, the lucky stiffs! While that was taking place, Flt Sgt Holmes and I were doing a dawn-to-dusk readiness at a nearby bomber base. The suffering and hardship we endured was not appreciated by our fellow pilots. In fact, they received with derision the story of our magnificent sacrifice of the comforts of our Mess and the harrowing tension of being the only two aircraft left to intercept the entire *Luftwaffe* if it came over. Of such stuff are martyrs made.

On the 23rd, the day set for the El Alamein offensive that was to decide the outcome of the war in the desert, Miluck noted:

Warned this morning that the big push begins at 2200hr tonight, supported by tanks and other equipment in sufficient numbers to form a two-to-one ratio in our favour. The Aussies are attacking from the north and the Anzacs joining them from the centre, leaving the south to the Indians.[69] Starting today, six Spitfires (!) are doing patrols over Daba to keep the *Luftwaffe* in the air. The CO says that once the push starts, our work will be easier. We hope so. After our daily pasting of El Daba and Fuka 'dromes, the *Luftwaffe* should be groggy.

Marting was missing this morning from a Wing bombing of Daba. They say he must have chased a 109.[70]

9.45 pm. Bags of excitement — everyone waiting for the guns to begin. What a bright, full moon tonight, by which to kill — or be killed.

10.00 pm. All hell has broken loose: 50 miles to the west, the horizon is filled with the man-made lightning of heavy artillery. As far back as this, the ground shakes and the tent walls quiver when the bombs fall.[71]

'At exactly 9.40pm the artillery opened with a terrific crash on the enemy gun positions and ammunition dumps ... air bombing of the positions added to the noise, and to the destruction wrought' (from Field Marshal Montgomery's account of El Alamein, written after revisiting the battlefield in 1967). From 9.55pm there was silence, then two searchlight beams swung skywards and intersected at 10pm, like crossed swords — the signal for the opening of 'a barrage of unimaginable intensity'

(*Alamein and the desert war, by Field Marshal Viscount Montgomery and others; Sphere Books, 1967*).

Hal Marting had taken off at 0700hr in a 239 Wing attack — 48 Kittyhawks — on El Daba airfield. With Sqn Ldr Dave Law leading 450 Sqn they flew northwards out over the blue Mediterranean, then turning westwards and heading for the spit of land (Ras Al Kanayis) which marked the Fuka area, then southwards towards their target. Although the Jerry guns along the Egyptian coast were out of range and everything seemed quiet and peaceful ... there wasn't a man of us ... who didn't know that a Messerschmitt could outrun, outclimb and outshoot us any day of the year. Our safety lay in sharp eyes, numbers and formation.[72]

Sqn Ldr Law gave the instruction 'Prepare to bomb ... prepare to bomb' as the tawny coastline and scattered buildings of El Daba came into view beneath them. Marting was one of six aircraft flying top cover, at 15,000ft. 'The bottom squadrons were too far below for us to watch them peel off for the dive, but we could hear the orders as each squadron went down in rotation. Flak was beginning to come up heavily, most of it aimed at the lower squadrons.'

'Lancer Squadron, get ready', came the quiet voice of Sqn Ldr Law. As the six top cover aircraft went into their dive they could see 'the four squadrons well over the target and almost vertical .... Tiny puffs of dust billowed up from the bombs of the fellows ahead of us.'

As we got into the flak, we could see the flashes from the guns around the airfield. Three aircraft were grouped on its near side, so I set my sights on them at 7,000ft, put a little back pressure on the control column and released my bomb. Bursts were thick all over the landing-ground by then: I didn't look to see where my bomb hit but pulled out of the dive.

The formation was slightly scattered by then. Weaving from side to side to keep them all in sight and still watch out for Jerries, I realized I was a little too far back for my liking and opened up the throttle fully. But nothing happened. I checked the instruments and pushed the propeller pitch control fully forward, into fine pitch. Again nothing happened. I couldn't figure out what was wrong, and never did. The engine sounded OK; all the instruments read correctly except for the manifold pressure[73] and airspeed, which had dropped to 200mph. As if I were standing still, the rest of the squadron went past me and in no time were fully a mile above and ahead of me. I was at 30,000ft, climbing with difficulty, and it was damned lonesome back there. A moment later my heart stopped. A thousand feet below, and dead ahead, four Me109s were climbing up. In a split second left to think, I figured they hadn't spotted me or they wouldn't be there; but it was a matter of another split second before they spotted me: then they would break formation and come in from all angles for the kill.

I stuck the nose down towards the nearest one and gave him a two-second burst from about 200 yards, closing to 75 yards. My shots hit him dead centre and he burst into flames, spiralling towards the ground. Pulling up and to the right, I started to squirt at the second one. All my guns fizzled out except the last one on the left, the few shots fired passing in front of his propeller as he turned up and away. The other two 109s were scrambling for the clouds, disorganized, not realizing there was only one of me. After a few more shots my last gun jammed. Figuring then that I was really in the wrong company, I rolled the aircraft on to its back then put the nose down, rolling in the dive until I got my bearings by the sun. The altimeter rapidly unwound — 7,000–5,000–3,000–1,000ft; just above the ground I levelled out, looking around for Jerries: by some freak of luck, none of them had followed me.

I headed east, keeping right on the deck and weaving all the time to keep a good lookout over my tail. There was the whole depth of the enemy lines to be crossed. My airspeed, which had gone up to 450 in the dive, soon dropped back to 235, but the engine was running smoothly and I thought I could make it back to LG175.

I dodged between some vehicles with open-mouthed soldiers standing by them and pushed the gun-button, without result. Dead ahead was a group of tanks and I pulled up a few feet to clear them.

The gun positions were getting more and more concentrated as I neared the front, and somebody must have 'phoned ahead to say that a lame duck was coming over. They began to open up with everything they had. I think those that didn't have guns were throwing up rocks.

Until that time, none of the aircraft I'd flown had been hit by an enemy shell. But now, above the noise of the engine, I heard the first shots connect — *splat, splat*, like a fly-swatter hitting a newspaper — and saw ragged holes appear in the wings. I zigzagged desperately. *Splat, splat* — those were in the tail: I felt a slight bounce as each one hit. Then a big noise deafened me and the cockpit was suddenly filled with the cordite fumes, smoke and glycol.

I switched off the fuel and ignition of what had once been an engine, wound back the cockpit cover and tightened my straps for the crash landing, trying to glide as far as possible with 10ft of altitude. Flak was still coming up like a blanket, but none of it hit me as I glided over the front lines. The aircraft touched down at about 100mph in a rough belly landing on the sand ridges, skidding to a stop after thirty yards or so.

As fast as I could, I got out of my 'chute and harness and climbed out to make sure the kite wasn't on fire. About ten Italian soldiers were already sprinting towards me with their tommy guns and there was no chance to run for it, especially in broad daylight, so I decided to be weak and willing. At least I was weak.

Notes to Chapter 2

1   No 239 Wing was then at LG91, Amirya: it had been formed on 24 April 1942 and had been at LG91 since 28 June.
2   Another fighter/bomber wing, No 233, had two squadrons of Tomahawks (Nos 4 and 5 (SAAF) and two of Kittyhawks (No 2 (SAAF) and No 260 (RAF)).
3   Spitfires, Hurricanes and Kittyhawks were ferried to Egypt up the West African Reinforcement Route from Takoradi, or from Port Sudan, and delivered first to Maintenance Units in the Canal Zone, where they were made ready for delivery to operational squadrons.
4   Which were electrically operated.
5   Flt Lt Carsons.
6   LG91.
7   The 'Kittybombers' specialized in ground-attack operations.
8   All the desert airfields were numbered: LG172 was SSW of Burg el Arab.

9 A South African who had been a Battle of Britain pilot with No 79 Sqn GDL Haysom had just been promoted Acting Wing Commander (on 22 July 1942) to lead No 239 Wing. He had been awarded the DFC in 1941.

10 I.e. the Qattara Depression.

11 In Palestine, a favourite leave centre for troops in the Middle East.

12 Sqn Ldr A.D. Ferguson, CO of 450 Sqn., RAAF, from May to October 1942.

13 The alternatives for leave were Alexandria or Palestine.

14 No 127 Sqn. — see previous note, p9.

15 Sqn Ldr C.O.J. Pegge, DFC, CO from 9 June 1942 to 21 April 1943. From June 1942 No 127 operated Hurricane IIBs.

16 One of Marting's sisters.

17 R.C. Ward was one of the Eagle Squadron pilots.

18 His wife and daughter.

19 Plt Off E.L. Sly, an Australian with whom Marting had done the shadow firing on the 15th. Fg Off J.W. Upward of No 3 (RAAF) Sqn, later killed in action on 17 November 1942.

20 Trade name for a phonograph — an early form of gramophone.

21 Westland Lysander, a high-wing monoplane capable of very short landing and take-off.

22 Famous for the 'sharks' teeth' with which the intakes of its Kittyhawks were painted.

23 Eight aircraft were scrambled on an armed recce over the forward area — at 1830hr, not in the morning.

24 This period was one of the worst for Allied fortunes, with the 8th Army bottled-up at El Alamein and the Russians desperately defending Stalingrad, their counter-offensive beginning on 19 November 1942 and ending with the surrender of the German 6th Army on 1 February 1943.

25 I.e. on No 450 Sqn, on No. 121 Sqn, which he had joined in August 1941, and on No 71 Sqn.

26 Recruits' centre near Warrington.

27 An Australian, Plt Off N.H. Shillabeer.

28 The latter operated by USAAF squadrons: see entry for 2 September. The Bostons were SAAF (South African Air Force) and the attack was on enemy transport.

29 Named after the Snyder Board, headed by Lt Col Alva W. Snyder, set up in 1942 to assess potential USAAF officer recruits (see *The Army Air Forces in World War II*, by W.F. Craven and J.L. Cate, Vol VI, Men and Planes — Office of Air Force History, 1983).

30 When he attempted to join the USAAC in 1940.

31 There were two squadrons at Deversoir — 81st and 82nd — and two at Ismailia — 83rd and 434th (Craven and Cate, Vol II, pp25–6).

32 Fran was his wife and Lennie (Lenore) his sister.

33 'OK' were the code letters for No 450 Sqn, 'A' the letter for Marting's own aircraft, EV160. This Kittyhawk IA had been delivered by sea to Alexandria aboard SS *Harperley*, arriving there on 17 May 1942 and being taken on charge on 31 August: hence its small number of hours — a test flight and delivery to the squadron.

34 This was a Wing operation; Miluck and Tribken were involved in a similar one later that day (1815hr–1845hr).

35 Westland Lysander, single-engined (890hp Bristol Mercury radial) high-wing monoplane designed for STOL (short take-off and landing) operations.

36 LG222, Fayoum Road, ten miles SSW of the Giza Pyramids.

37 These 'throat mikes' differed from the RAF ones, which were combined with the oxygen mask.

38 'Five plus Stukas with 109s as cover were attacked' (squadron ORB).

39 R.D. Dyson and D.H. McBurnie were pilots on 450 Sqn.

40 The missing pilots were Plt Off Donald and Sgt Scribner of 3 Sqn, Sgt Young of 112, Plt Of Thorpe and Sgt Strong of 250 and Sgt Ewing of 450 (No 239 Wing ORB).

41 Nicknamed 'The Chief' because of his Sioux Indian descent.

42 The Bristol Bombay, a twin-engined, high wing bomber/transport which had served in the Middle East since September 1939.

43 Most of the bars in Cairo had suitably 'patriotic' names, which would have been quickly changed if the Afrika Korps broke through El Alamein and the German/Italian forces arrived there.

44 Nomis was on 229 Sqn at Ta Kali, Malta, from 12 August to 14 September 1942 and then with 92 Sqn in the Western Desert from 14 November 1942. Writing about his Malta experience after the war (see Vern Haugland's *The Eagle Squadrons Yanks in the RAF 1940–42*; Ziff Davis Flying Books, 1979) he said that those posted there 'should have been awarded a medal for the mere arriving .... I have never been to another place with such a visible atmosphere of doom, violence and toughness about it. ... Coming out from England as we did, the filth, flies, diseases and near starvation absolutely fascinated us, the more so because the interception missions ... were not in the least deterred by these handicaps. The air war seemed more deadly here, the 109s more sinister than the 190s of northern France .... A lot of the Eagles, some of whom were seemingly clueless in England, ran up their scores and got their gongs in Malta. Not speaking for myself, because I was involved in more farces than victories .... Malta either made or broke them.'

45 By the end of the war, 46 ex-members of 71 Sqn had been killed in action or on active service. In all, 107 out of the 240 Eagle Squadron pilots lost their lives during the war.

46 The 66th Fighter Squadron was part of the 57th Fighter Group, which operated with No 239 Wing: it had P-40s (see Craven & Cate, Vol II, pp 25-27).

47 Junkers Ju 87 Stuka (Sturzkampflugzeug) dive-bomber, with its 'cranked' wing of 45ft 3.5in span and fixed, spatted undercarriage, had been spectacularly successful in the blitzkrieg of 1940 but was no match for contemporary fighters.

48 I.e. line-shooting, in which all aircrew indulged when they had nothing better to do.

49 Sqn Ldr R.D. Mannix, OC No 33 Sqn: see previous note.

50 Trenchard had been CAS briefly in 1918, before taking command of the Independent Force in France, then from 1919 to 1929 when his main work of establishing the RAF was done. He was subsequently Commissioner of the Metropolitan Police, retiring in 1934 at the age of 63, so he would have been 70 at the time of his visit to the Middle East in 1942.

51 A desynchronized note which became all too familiar to people in Britain during the Luftwaffe's night raids.

52 Nicknamed 'Mary' (i.e. 'Maori' — a reference to his New Zealand nationality), AVM Andrew Coningham was AOC Desert Air Force.

53 Coningham's opposite number in the Luftwaffe (see previous note).

54 "Four Wing escorts to Baltimore and Mitchell aircraft bombing enemy landing grounds. Wing fighters strafed these landing grounds after the bombing" (No 239 Wing ORB, 9 October).

55 The Macchi C.202 was probably the Regia Aeronautica's best fighter: it had a German (Daimler-Benz) engine.

56 Its 14 Kittyhawks got to LG91 at 0740hr, two more arriving later.

57 One of the original RAF airfields in Egypt, close to Cairo.

58 Flt Lt McR Shepperd was the Squadron Adjutant and Flt Lt Matthews the Equipment Officer: these films were presumably taken in May 1942 when the squadron was at Gambut, before it withdrew to El Daba and then to LG91.

59   No 462 Sqn, RAAF, was then the Halifax squadron at Fayid.
60   Re-conditioned Allison engines were likely to seize up because of bearings failure.
61   Martin B-26 Marauders began to appear in the Middle East in mid-1942, No. 14 Sqn being the first RAF squadron to operate them.
62   The Battle of El Alamein started on the night of 23 October 1942, as will be seen.
63   Plt Off D.W. Cairns, a very experienced DAF pilot.
64   Prior to the Battle of El Alamein, the Desert Air Force had three Wings of fighter-bombers (14 squadrons including the two attached USAAF squadrons, the 64th and 66th), two Wings of fighters (eight squadrons) and two Wings of light bombers (seven squadrons including the USAAF 81st Bombardment Squadron).
65   Author of the classic account of the days of the Chinese warlords, *Leaf in the Storm*, (Lythway, 1974).
66   Service bankers in the Middle East.
67   Plt Off G.W. Troke.
68   Plt Off J.R. Falconer-Taylor, missing from this operation, subsequently 'walked back' (see later entry).
69   In Montgomery's plan for the battle, the 9th Australian Division was to attack in the north, the 51st Highland Division plus 1st Armoured Division in the 'northern corridor', and 2nd New Zealand Division plus 9th Armoured Brigade plus 10th Armoured Division in the 'southern corridor', with 1st South African Division and 4th Indian Division on the southern flank. Fighting went on for 12 days before the break-out was achieved.
70   In the afternoon of the 23rd (1530–1650hr) Miluck was one of twelve 250 Sqn Kittyhawks which made a sweep over El Daba – no enemy aircraft being encountered.
71   'The night of October 23 was clear, with a brilliant moon. As zero hour approached we heard the bombers flying overhead to play their part in the conflict.' *(Australia in the War of 1939–45. Vol II).*
72   This account of his last operation was written by Marting in January 1943, after his return from captivity.
73   I.e. Boost gauges indicating engine power.

Fg Off Miluck in his Kittyhawk — showing three of its
six 0.5in machine-guns.

Kittyhawk of No 250 Sqn about to take off.

A Kittyhawk landing at LG91: the 40 gal oil drums were used
as runway markers.

Sqn Ldr Hancock after returning in his damaged Kittyhawk.
The 250 Sqn identification letters LD can be seen.

CHAPTER 3
PoW

So ended the Battle of El Alamein for Hal Marting — on the day before it started, down on the wrong side of the lines and about to become a PoW. He 'didn't bother to put up his hands' as the Italians approached. They knew he would have a revolver — all aircrew carried them on operations — but, heavily outnumbered, he 'probably didn't look much like a candidate for suicide'. While two of the soldiers covered him with their guns, 'the others took my parachute, helmet, revolver, Mae West and everything else removable, for souvenirs. One of them indicated that he wanted my wrist watch. I indicated that I wanted to keep it. He cocked his gun and I almost broke my wrist getting it off.'

It seemed to me that they were taking a devil of a time and I was suddenly very thirsty.

'Aqua', I said, making a motion of raising a flask to my lips. They let me get a water bottle out of the tail of the aircraft.

As we headed westwards, I saw that I'd missed their minefields by only about eight feet, the Kittyhawk's tail raking the barbed wire as it passed over. Fuses were sticking up through the sand as thick as buttercups. That didn't help my nerves much. My captors showed me where to walk — very carefully.

The CO of the 62nd Italian Infantry had his HQ in a dugout at the rear end of a truck.

'The Colonel demands to know', interpreted an Intelligence officer after I'd been marched in, 'why America makes war on Italy'.

'Tell the Colonel I demand to know why Italy made war on France and Greece', I responded.

The Colonel didn't seem to like me; in fact he shook with rage.

'Africa is no place for Americans and English!'

'I agree heartily!'

'Africa is for Italians!'

'Tell the Colonel', I said to the IO, 'that Africa is a good place for Africans!'

It was good to get back into the car with the guards.

Just before sunset we arrived at El Daba railway station, where the driver had to ask where the PoW camp was located. Then we drove a mile back along the road to a guardhouse with a barbed-wire enclosure behind it, near the railway line. In return for a written receipt the Italians handed me over, like a parcel or a piece of luggage, to the Jerries.

Instead of putting me in the enclosure, the two officers in charge motioned for me to sit down. I sat on the ground, leaning against the guardhouse, while they heated some canned stew on a small petrol stove and opened some canned pears. Not bad, I thought, when I noticed they were dividing the food into three equal portions. It came as a pleasant shock when they handed one of the pans to me.

'Thanks', I said, and they smiled at the surprise in my voice.

'The *dummkopf* Italians to the wrong camp brought you,', one of them managed to convey. 'To the *Luftwaffe* camp you must go.'

Darkness fell while we were eating. The stew was good; it even had a little meat in it. Beyond the barbed wire, where a German sentry paced with his rifle, I caught an occasional dim glimpse of British and American uniforms. An engine chugged past on the railway track and from far overhead came the drone of an aircraft. I hoped that a certain Australian squadron wouldn't have as its next morning's target railway station 'X', El Daba.

When a relief officer arrived I got into a German car — a Volkswagen 'people's car', designed for pleasure motoring in the Fatherland but now fallen on sorrier days — with one of the officers who had fed me. We were driven to the *Luftwaffe* HQ, a big tent half buried in sand dunes on the beach near the airfield we'd bombarded that morning, with palm trees rustling round it in the night breeze.

Inside it, five men in khaki shirts and shorts were gathered round a table, their faces etched sharply in the light of a lantern. Individually, they were as unlike as any five Americans who might be thrown together by circumstances, but immediately I felt their close kinship for one another and my own alienation. These men were German.

'For you the war is now finished', grinned a young lieutenant with a thin, sharp face and bristling sandy hair.

'All finished!' Another jolly fellow slapped me on the back. He was an ox of a man with a square head and a round, rather simple face, who looked as if he seldom thought of anything but *schnapps* and *Wienerschnitzel*; but something told me he was the cleverest and most dangerous of the lot.

'What is the use to keep fighting?' he asked, smiling. 'Do you know how many British 'planes were shot down yesterday? — 62!'

'Propaganda', I replied, shortly. I knew, as a matter of fact, that we had lost 11.

'No, no — 62', he persisted. He produced a paper and showed me a list of names of fellows who were, or had been, in my squadron and pointed to several of them. 'These are prisoners. And these are dead'.

'Look: you're wasting time', I said.

But they must have had plenty of it to waste, for they kept it up for hours. At eleven o'clock they walked me under the stars to a small barbed-wire enclosure and put me in a tent that already had several occupants. Three very thin mattresses were pulled together on the ground and there was a blanket for each of us. The guard took away my boots[1], in case I had any idea of escaping, promising to return them to me in the morning.

'Here comes another one', said a good mid-Western American voice, and I heard the other occupants stirring under their blankets. I couldn't see them and they couldn't see me.

'You wouldn't happen to be a Hoosier?'[2] I said to the voice.

'Ohio', he replied.

'When did you get in?'

'This morning. They got us with flak. We're part of a bomber crew.'

'Bale out?'

'Two of the gunners did. The rest of us belly-landed.'

'Shut-up', said another voice. 'He may be a ringer.'[3]

Afraid that I was a Jerry put there to get information, they talked very little after that. We huddled up together to keep warm.

It had been a very long day for Hal Marting. Recording its attacks on El Daba airfield that day, No 450 Sqn noted in its Operations Record Book: 'J4919 Fg Off H.F. Marting is missing from this operation'.[4]

From now on, the fortunes of the two Eagles diverged: Marting, held at El Daba, was interviewed by a German war correspondent — Count von Eckstadt; Miluck was flying top cover to 112 and 66 Sqns, 'up in the lonely six' — very unhappy and squirming in his seat, noting in his diary: 'what an uncomfortable feeling to be flying at full throttle and see the others slowly pull ahead of you. To make it worse, my No 2 (Flt Sgt Holmes) had a kite whose speed was about the same as mine, and he was supposed to weave more and watch my tail. He says he can spot me by my weaving, because it's more violent than most. The harder to hit, my dear'. [The ORB of 250 Sqn records: '0730–0825hr escort to Baltimores and Mitchells. Bombing 6 miles south of Al-El-Rahman. No e/a seen'.]

Slept straight through until sunrise, when the guard brought us some good brown bread and some ersatz coffee which tasted strongly of chlorine. Our boots were returned a little later. Without tooth brushes, razors, soap or water, we simply sat around and looked one another over: Jim Cleary from Columbus, Ohio; Francis Finnegan from Buffalo, NY; and Bill O'Berg from River, Michigan — all with the US Army Air Corps.

As far as convincing them that I wasn't a Jerry they might all have been from Missouri. I named streets, buildings and hotels from Seattle to Tampa, recited facts and figures until I was hoarse.

'Look, fellows', said Jim Cleary at last. 'No-one but a lousy Hoosier could talk like that!' We got quite friendly!

In the afternoon the guard brought in a fourth member of the bomber crew, who had bailed out — McMahan, from the state of Washington — and later we acquired another cell-mate, a South African named Corson. He spoke German well and had acquired the information that we were leaving the next morning by truck for Tobruk, from where we would be flown to Greece. Of the five other occupants of our PoW camp I knew only one — Hogg, a Canadian. All, of course, were aircrew.

On this second morning (24 October) we were all feeling pretty ropey and were in much need of toothbrushes. My personal tragedy was that I had no handkerchief: I'd never before realised the multitude of uses for a plain white square of cloth. At dawn we were told to get ready to leave.

A compass and a map of the desert showing water holes had been buried under the mattress by a former inmate who hadn't had time to dig them up again, and I put the map in the top of one boot and pulled my trouser leg over it. The compass I kept in my pocket.

A truck driven by an officer arrived, and the six of us climbed into the back with six guards. Each of us was given an overcoat to wear over our other clothing, and a big box of food was put in for the journey. The guards had their baggage and were going back to Germany on leave, which made them considerably happier than we felt and looked. Only one of them could speak English — Fritz Eiban, a handsome boy of 20 who came from a small island off the north coast of Germany. A schoolteacher before the war, he was now a corporal in the *Luftwaffe*.

Just beyond Mersa Matruh[5], two Army officers stopped the truck and climbed in: they were also going home on leave. One of them addressed us arrogantly. 'If you damned Yankees had not come into the war,' he said, 'it would have been over by now.'

Some time later he took great pleasure in taking my map away from me. Sitting with my legs stretched out, my trousers had crept up over the top of my boots and a corner of the map had worked its way out. I tried to cover it with my hand but he caught me doing so.

At Sidi Barrani we stopped by the roadside for lunch, then pushed on to Gambut, arriving late at night. Gambut was not a town — merely a stopping-place, one lone building out in the sand and camel grass. It was one of those nights peculiar to the desert, of a velvety blackness without moon or stars, when you couldn't see anything more than six feet away from you. Cleary and I looked hopefully and hopelessly at one another. We could make a break and lose ourselves in that blackness before the guards knew what was happening — if only we had that map showing the water-holes. Without it, there would be just six more corpses on the sands of the desert. We shivered through the night on a tiled floor without mattresses or blankets.

Tobruk came into sight at about 8 o'clock the next morning (27 October). We breakfasted at a canteen on the outskirts and went on to the airfield, where our guards booked passages on an aircraft leaving at about noon. Here were all the familiar activities of an aerodrome — aircraft taking off and landing, being loaded and unloaded; passengers, baggage and drums of fuel — with one nightmarish difference: the aircraft had big black crosses on them instead of red, white and blue roundels, and the shouts of air crew and ground crew were guttural-sounding.

Our aircraft was a Ju 52 transport[6]. Besides the six of us, eighteen Germans climbed aboard and sat on the luggage along the sides. All of them were armed, and we gave up our vague hope of seizing the controls and making our way back to the Allied lines.

We landed on Crete to refuel, taking off again immediately and reaching an airfield north-west of Athens just as the sun was setting. Corson learned from the guards that we were to stay in Athens overnight and take a train in the morning for Frankfurt, where there was a PoW transit centre.

The Hotel Rex was a small establishment in the down-town area of Athens — six of us and seven guards took up the whole of the third floor, two prisoners and one guard in each of three rooms, three guards in another one, and the remaining guard sharing a room with an officer we hadn't seen before.

We cheered up a little at the sight of beds and clean sheets. Better still, there was running water. We hadn't washed or shaved for four days, nor had anything to drink except for the stuff they called coffee. We borrowed razors from the guards, bathed, and slept that night like dead men.[7]

* * * * *

On 25 October Miluck was on a long-range sweep — 'looking for trouble, but nothing happened until we started home. Then one of the new pilots became separated. Suddenly the radio crackled and a voice yelled. "Help! Help! I'm being attacked by 109s. Help!" Since we were at 8,000ft and he was away behind and below on the deck, it was useless to try to locate him, so we continued home. A few seconds later, "For Christ's sake, help me! The bastards are on my tail!" We stooged on. Finally, someone drawled: "Have you bought it yet?" He got back boiling mad, but very willing to keep in formation in future'. [The 250 Sqn ORB records for 25 October: 'Top cover to twelve Baltimores and six Mitchells.

112 Sqn leading bombing 864304. No e/a encountered. 200 MT seen well dispersed.' Miluck's sortie was 1100–1205hr].

That night there was a sandstorm at LG91 — 'just like the snow blizzards that you read about. Sand in your ears and eyes and mouth, gritting every time you take a bite'. Miluck found it impossible to see his tent — fifty yards from the Mess — but 'fixed that by tying a guide rope between them'. He drank a lime juice, keeping his hand cupped over the glass, 'but a quarter-inch of sand soon settled in the bottom anyway. Most of us keep handkerchiefs tied round our faces like desperados, and the only time we have our caps off is when we sleep. The powdery stuff floats through the air, settling on everything, sifting into the cockpits and covering the floor of the aircraft. Wally did a slow roll today and claims he had to come out on instruments'.

On the 26th, Wing Commander G.D.L. Haysom told his pilots at LG91 that the *Luftwaffe* had 'bought it' as a result of the pre-Alamein air offensive. 'We damaged 120 aircraft in the Daba-Fuka bombings', Miluck noted. 'When the Jerries arrive in their brand-new kites as reinforcements, to find a bombed and strafed 'drome and a warm reception from the RAF, they won't be such eager beavers. The plan is to keep Spitfires over their 'dromes all day and at the same time maintain a constant shuttle service over enemy lines, bombing and strafing motor transport, keeping the remaining 109s and 202s in the air and wearing-down their serviceability. Each of us averages four shows a day — about 90 minutes each trip'. [On the 26th, according to the 250 Sqn ORB, Miluck was on an afternoon sortie — 1628–1740hr — top cover to 112 Sqn dive-bombing LG20, six bombed-up and six as top cover].

* * * * *

Noting a personal unserviceability, Miluck commented ruefully that he'd been 'doing a small shuttle service' of his own since 4 am, 'to and from our "Desert Lily".[8] Damned gypo-gut[9] from fly-infested food. Was almost sick in the air, but compromised with a spinning head'.

That day, Fg Off Falconer-Taylor 'walked casually into the Mess after crash-landing in enemy territory and walking more than 90 miles in three days with a broken hand'.[10]

Marting was in Greece, a PoW; Miluck, at LG91, was still involved in the El Alamein battle. On 27 October he was 'up again in the middle of the night for another dawn show [not according to the ORB: he was on 1200–1320hr]. Same old story: the leader of our six got left miles behind in the turn. Thank God no Jerry kites saw us or we'd still be dog-fighting. Our group today got 15 destroyed, four probables and four damaged, all for the loss of three Kittyhawks.' He spared a thought for the ground crew, refuelling, re-arming and servicing the aircraft on the dusty desert airfield:

> At four shows a day, our ground crews have to work damned hard, so I bought mine several beers each to show my appreciation. Since we're rationed to three cans a day, at 35¢ a can, I couldn't do more. Mine is one of the best and most experienced crews in the desert. What I do reflects on them: if I shoot down an enemy aircraft, they've also shot it down.

* * * * *

That morning, Marting and his fellow PoWs were taken for a walk through the streets of Athens while train reservations were made for their onward journey to Frankfurt. These streets, on the morning of 27 October 1942, appeared to Marting's eyes to be

> narrow, winding and hilly, the buildings low and crowded, and the signs on them 'all Greek' to us; but the air was sharp and clean. We soon had to turn back, however, as such a crowd of Greeks was following us that traffic was blocked. Several of these people threw cigarettes to us, smiled and made 'V' signs. Our guards were furious. The one who had gone to the station came back with the news that we would have to wait five days

for a train. This was a blow to the Jerries who were going on leave, but it suited me fine.

Though confined to the third floor and eating our meals out of the box of food we had brought along, we were treated well. The guards let us use their toilet articles and even bought coffee and extra food for us out of their own pockets. During the day we were kept together in one of the rooms across the front of the building; at night I slept with Finnegan and Fritz Eiban in a room at the back, next to the guards' room. The window looked out on a small court completely surrounded by three- and four-storey buildings, except in one spot. One building had a narrow extension to it, one storey high, leaving an opening two feet wide above the roof. I couldn't see where it led.

Fritz caught me looking at it one day. 'No, no', he said reprovingly. 'I wouldn't like that at all. If any of you escape I shall spend two years in prison.'

We cooked up a scheme for all of us to escape, the idea being to knock off the guards when there were only two of them left with us. Corson and I were then to put on their uniforms and march the others out for their 'walk', Corson doing any talking necessary.

* * * * *

At El Alamein the battle which was to decide the outcome of the Middle East war was now entering its sixth day and its decisive stage. On 29 October the Kittyhawk squadrons of No 239 Wing carried out ground strafing attacks and interception patrols and provided escorts to Baltimores and Mitchells bombing the 15th Panzers. During these operations, the ORB noted: 'One Ju 88, two He111s and one Me109, plus one staff car carrying officers, were destroyed; and two Ju 86s, one Me109, 20MT vehicles, one AA post and numerous tents were damaged. All our aircraft returned safely'.

The No 250 Sqn ORB recorded that in the morning of that day (1020hr to 1135hr) twelve aircraft led by Flt Lt Barber took off as top cover to 112 Sqn who were to bomb the Daba landing-grounds. The formation flew out over the coast, turning in towards the land when east of Daba and bombing east to west. Bombs were dropped on both LG20 and LG104.[11] Top cover was at 16,000–18,000ft and very little ack-ack was experienced at this height. No enemy aircraft were seen in the air. After bombing both squadrons patrolled the central sector, returning home on orders from the Controller.

The ORB then described that afternoon's (1420–1630hr) operations:

Our major effort today was a long-range strafing flight by twelve of our aircraft in two sixes. Flt Lt Barber led one six to Mersa Matruh junction where a goods train was shot up, together with MT and boxed stores in the sidings. Flt Lt Barber destroyed a staff car on the road and damaged further MT and trucks.... Ft Lt Hancock led the other six to Mersa Matruh aerodrome and found seven aircraft on the ground. Of these, two He111s and one Ju 86 were destroyed and two further Ju 86s badly damaged. MT and tents were also effectively strafed and many a Hun badly scared.... The route out was over the sea, making a landfall at Ras El Alam El Rum and parting into flights there. The two flights joined up again about fifteen miles south of target and came back together via the Depression, [flying at] 500 to 1,000ft all the way....

Miluck was on both operations, in the morning

...up in the lonely six again, watching 112 Sqn dive-bomb a landing-ground. Sat at 20,000ft for over an hour, and Kittyhawks just barely wallow through the air at that altitude.[12] Talk about having the nervous twitch! Returning from target, we did a fighter sweep over the lines, looking for 109s, but couldn't find any....

To his account of the afternoon 'op' he added a homely note:

> Later in the day the squadron did a 'strafe' at Mersa Matruh, never flying more than 200ft from the deck. Came in from the sea, surprised an aerodrome and destroyed at least three 'planes and damaged others before running for home.
>
> Mailed Christmas cards to the States, including one to Mother and one to a popsy in London. Rather worried. Haven't heard from Mother in months, and not at all from that piece of fluff in London. What is it my friends haven't told me?

On the morning of 30 October — sixth day of the battle of El Alamein — No 250 Sqn provided top cover for an escort to bombers attacking Fuka. On the return, the ORB noted, four Me109s appeared: 'Plt Off Stewart turned his flight about into them, firing at [one of them] without visible results. The 109s sheered off and top cover re-formed and returned to base without further incident. Results of bombing were difficult to observe owing to cloud which was ten-tenths in places.'

Miluck recorded in his diary:

> Still another show to Fuka, again on top, covering twelve Baltimores and six Mitchells .... As we turned for home and broke cloud at 1,000ft, I spotted and reported three 109s at five o'clock; but they wouldn't play, and we couldn't leave the bombers, so no one had any fun.

No 250 Sqn did three operations that day and Miluck was also on the third (1625–1725hr) — close escort to eighteen Baltimores bombing enemy concentrations in the northern sector, the Kittyhawks also carrying bombs. The pilots, according to the ORB, did not see much of their target or the results of their bombing — visibility was very poor over the target and out to sea, but the Army 'reported that the bombing was most satisfactory'. Miluck seemed to have no doubts about his personal success, recording in his diary:

> ... did a dusk show, bombing motor transport in the northern sector, and was pleased to see my bomb splash a big, fat truck. Returned in time to hear Air Marshal Tedder[13] give out with some genuine dope on the push. Everyone full of confidence. I was, too, until he told us about the new 109Gs[14] arriving from Sicily, armed with four 20mm cannon. Think I'll ask for some leave.

Notes to Chapter 3

 1 Marting was wearing riding-boots and KD slacks when he was shot down.
 2 A native of Indiana.
 3 An imposter or informer.
 4 No 239 Wing recorded in its ORB for 23 October 1942: '131 sorties were made during fighter bombing attacks and offensive sweeps. Two 109Fs were destroyed for the loss of one of our pilots.'
 5 About 70 miles westward along the coast road from El Daba.
 6 Three-engined, this Junkers civil/military transport had a distinctive 'corrugated iron' appearance.
 7 Marting's account of his experiences as a PoW appeared in *The American Magazine* in August 1943.
 8 Colloquial name for 'conveniences' in the desert.
 9 Otherwise known as 'Gippy-tummy', a form of dysentery common in the desert.
10 A special award, whose emblem was a winged flying-boot, was instituted for those who 'walked back' — thus qualifying for membership of the 'Late Arrivals Club', as Marting did.
11 Landing-grounds in the El Daba area.
12 Lack of a good operational 'ceiling' was one of the reasons for the Kittyhawk's limited success as an intercepter, but it was successful as a ground-attack fighter-bomber aircraft.
13 AOC-in-C, Middle East Air Force.
14 No 250 Sqn had encountered them on the 26th: 'These e/a were reported as 109Gs, having the mainplane set back further along the fuselage than the E or F variety.'

CHAPTER 4
Escape

That same afternoon, far from the dust and smoke of the desert battle, Hal Marting was about to begin his own private war with the Axis forces — his escape and evasion through Greece and into Turkey. But there was a long way and a long time (two months) to go, and it was only his fitness, his experience and his determination which saw him through on this fourth day in Athens:

They told us we would leave for Germany the next morning as guests of the Führer. At three o'clock that afternoon, only two guards were on duty — one of them in the officers' room listening to the radio, Fritz apparently asleep in the guards' room. The other fellows promised to cover my absence as long as possible by saying that I'd gone to the toilet.

I said goodbye to them, sneaked into my bedroom and locked the door. When opening the window I noticed that Fritz had left his bag on the old iron bed. I went to work on the lock with a nail file. By some miracle it came open. I found myself breathing like a racehorse. Inside the bag were a pair of Jerry trousers that buckled at the ankles and a *Luftwaffe* cap — no coat. I had only my British khaki shirt. I put on the trousers and cap, opened the window and climbed out on to the fire escape.

In the sunlight that illuminated half the court, it seemed to me that I stood out like a sore thumb against the side of that hotel. The windows of the surrounding buildings stared back at me like lifeless eyes. My heart pounded until I was breathless and sick, and so clumsy that the heels of my boots rasped in the silence across the edges of the iron steps.

As I passed the second floor a woman put her head out of the window, starting to speak. I motioned her to be quiet: she withdrew hurriedly and closed the window. Would she raise an alarm? Yes, I thought dully, for a light came on in the first floor hall that opened on to the court. I reached the ground and flattened myself against the wall in a corner. At last the light went off. I ducked across the court towards that two-foot strip of freedom 12ft above the ground.

There was an old table in the corner, with wobbly legs. I got it into position below the drain pipe and climbed on to it. Then, with one foot on the pipe, I pulled myself up until I could grip the roof with the fingers of one hand. The pipe broke away from the wall with a sickening clatter, and pure terror must have propelled me up to the roof. A few feet back from the court, the wall on my right ended and I jumped down into another small court, behind a building on the next street. From there I got into the main hallway and entered the first door I came to.

At first I thought my prayer for less conspicuous clothing had been answered, for I found myself in a tailor's shop. Then I noticed that the owner was standing defensively behind his counter and that there was fear in the eyes of an elderly man there. They were staring at my *Luftwaffe* cap.

I pointed to it quickly and shook my head. 'American-English', I said. I pointed to a suit hanging on the rack and made a beckoning gesture. The tailor spoke angrily, waving me towards the door, and another precious thirty seconds were wasted before I realized that he wouldn't help me.

I went back to the street entrance, drew a deep breath and walked out. I kept on walking; block after block was put behind me, and though I passed a number of Italian soldiers I encountered no Jerries. After thirty minutes or so I found myself in a residential district.

Rounding a corner, I stopped short. Ahead was a public park, with a whole company of Jerries standing to attention. They saw me but they didn't break ranks, and the officer in charge of the parade had his back towards me. I spun round on my heel and got away from there as fast as I could without running.

The Greeks I passed in the street seemed to have a complete disregard for everything German, including my 'uniform' — cap and trousers. Only one pair of eyes met mine — those of a man standing at the kerb. In a flash it seemed that there was something familiar about him, something as hauntingly familiar as a memory out of a dream, but I couldn't stop to figure it out.

I must have passed several blocks before I realized that someone was following me. I could hear footsteps coming along steadily behind me, always gaining a little, but I felt too paralyzed to turn round and look. I went down a side street. The footsteps followed. The only thing to do, I decided, was to let him overtake me, give him a quick one-two and run for it. I slowed down.

At last he was walking beside me, an emaciated fellow in civilian clothing. He'd taken off his hat and the minute I saw his hair — streaked with gold as if the sun had burnished it — I remembered. He'd been in the crowd that had followed us, that first day when we went for a walk. But when he asked me a question in German I didn't know what to do. If he were a German agent ....

He repeated the question in Greek. I was tongue-tied.

Then he changed to French: '*Qu'avez-vous, monsieur?*' — 'Are you in trouble?'

I liked his face and the way he spoke. 'Yes' I, said.

'How long have you been in the *Luftwaffe*?'

'About an hour and a half, and the quicker I get out of it, the better.'

'Where are you going?'

'I'm on my way to the country.'

'Come with me. I will show you the way.'

We walked for another twenty minutes; then he turned into a block of flats and we climbed up several flights of stairs, to a small flat on the top floor. It was comfortably furnished, and there were a number of books, magazines and papers in several languages. He gave me a cigarette and lighted it for me.

'Who are you?'

'Flying Officer H.F. Marting, J4919, Royal Canadian Air Force. An American in British service, shot down in Egypt.'

'Yes?' His voice was cool. 'How came you by the cap and trousers?'

'Stole them from the guard.'

Obviously he had to be convinced, and he put me through an interrogation to check my identity. When he was satisfied, I asked: 'How far do they search when anyone escapes?'

'It is possible that they might search here.'

'Let me go away until it's over. I'll come back. If they find me here .... It's not only your own safety', I added with sudden realization, 'it's your family, your relatives — you can't endanger them'.

He smiled grimly — 'You're right. I can't endanger them. They're all dead.'

I sat down slowly. 'But even if they don't find me now', I said, 'they may trace me later. If anything should happen to you after I've gone, I would never know about it.'

'Nothing will happen to me after you've gone, because I'm going with you. My time here is about finished. We must wait a while; then we will go.'

'What is your name, sir?' I asked.

'Names are unimportant in times like these, Lieutenant; living is all that matters. For the present, call me Bill.'

The man-hunt lasted about three days, Bill told me later. I saw and heard nothing of it. Naturally it was kept very quiet — and so was I — in the bedroom of the flat. For food, he brought me a bowl of plain boiled rice. He also brought me some civilian clothes which had belonged to a man who had been shot two days before by the Germans — an old shirt and coat, trousers with the seat out of them, a battered hat. That night I burned Fritz Eiban's trousers, along with my British shirt, and buried his *Luftwaffe* cap, wondering how he liked being in jail.

For shoes I had to keep the English riding-boots I was wearing when shot down, with my trousers pulled down over them.

Marting's civilian clothes were provided by a widow — Angela Melidi — whose husband had been shot by the Germans for his Resistance activities. She also helped in the change of his appearance which he subsequently described.

Her name became known after the war when she wrote to his sister Lenore (Mrs Don Silvers) in March 1946 enclosing the diary he had kept while in Athens. Many years later Mrs Silvers said in a newspaper interview:[1]

Angela Melidi[2] hid my brother for 12 days, moving him from place to place — including a coal bin — and giving him her husband's clothes, dyeing his hair and moustache and providing what food she could for his 'walk'.

'Bill', who led the group of evaders out of Greece, was a prominent Greek Army officer whose name I do not know. He had gone underground and the Germans were so hot on his trail he needed to get out of the country for a while.

* * * * *

At El Alamein the battle had now reached a crucial stage — the break-out which would send the 8th Army advancing westwards in pursuit of the Afrika Korps.

On 31 October, No 239 Wing noted that 200 sorties had been made on armed reconnaissances, ground strafing attacks and bomber escorts; a Stuka 'party' had been successfully intercepted by No 112 Sqn with the result that five Ju 87s and two Me109s had been destroyed, four 109Fs, one Ju 87 and one Me202 probably destroyed, and four Me109Fs and four Ju 87s damaged. Strafing attacks had resulted in four petrol-carrying MT vehicles and five other MTs being destroyed, and 41 MT vehicles, 11 ammunition dumps and one gun-carrier damaged. Such was the scale of destruction wrought upon the Afrika Korps by the Kittyhawk squadrons.

No 250 recorded in its ORB that at 0720hr that day eleven aircraft took off as top cover to 112 Sqn

> Kitty bombing concentration of tents and MT. ... On leaving the target they were ordered to patrol Northern Area. We remained as top cover at a height of 18–19,000ft. Soon after patrol commenced, six Me202s were seen coming west and our formation turned into them. Flt Lt Taylor shot at one of the Macchis and saw his bullet strikes along its fuselage. Before these M202s could be attacked six Me109s were seen coming out of the sun and the formation was turned into them. Flt Lt Hancock, Fg Off Calver, Fg Off Whiteside, Flt Sgt Graham and Sgt Baron all put in bursts at the enemy aircraft. Fg Off Whiteside claims his 109F was probably destroyed. On return to base it was found that these enemy fighters were part of an escort to Stukas which had been bombing our forward positions. While we had remained above and kept the fighters busy, 112 Sqn had been able to go down and deal with the Stukas, destroying two of them.

Ed Miluck was on this operation, as he wrote in his diary.

> ... Seeing patchy cloud cover at 10,000ft, I knew what to expect — and the expected happened. ... Over the target, three 109s flying line astern attacked from seven o'clock and we did a turnabout into them. Continued the turn into a 360° circle like a damned merry-go-round, with the 109s flying on the outside, just out of range. I fired a futile burst anyway. All the way home, dirty darts were made from five to seven o'clock, and finally a lucky burst from 500 yards by a Macchi 202 damaged Sgt Stephens' kite, but he crash-landed OK on our side of the lines.

Apparently being in a Desert Air Force squadron had occasional compensations, even at the height of a major battle. The cooks had done their best for the returning pilots, Miluck noting: '250 Sqn's Grill Room had a very savoury lunch waiting for us — sliced tomatoes, mashed potatoes with tomato cream sauce, sausage patties and biscuits, all washed down with hot black coffee.'

That day he also recorded in his diary that Marting's CO (Sqn Ldr J.E.A. Williams) had gone missing:

> In the excitement of an attack by Macchi 202s on a long range strafe at Sidi Barrani, the Commanding Officer of 450 Sqn was shot down by his own No 2. He force-landed OK but is a hell of a long way from home. Guess I'll buy my No 2 some drinks![3]

* * * * *

During the early November days before the squadrons moved forward from El Alamein in the wake of the advancing 8th Army, Hal Marting lay low in Athens before his own break-out could be achieved — into the uncertainties of escape and evasion in the wild and mountainous Greek countryside. First, he was cooped up in the small flat where he had been taken, until it was safe for him to be moved out:

> I dyed my hair, eyebrows and moustache a horrible black, but shaved off my moustache after seeing it in a mirror: there are limits to human credibility. Each day I had to scrape my face closely with a dull razor blade to avoid showing a blonde stubble, and my skin became raw and red. As the crowning touch to my new identity I forged Greek identification papers similar to Bill's and had my photograph taken by a street photographer to paste-in on them. But I still had to keep under cover most of the time because I looked so well fed. The best time to move around was in the early hours of the night before eleven o'clock. After that time, anyone found on the streets was automatically stopped and questioned.

On the third night [3 November] Bill moved me to a small house and hid me in an empty coal bin in the cellar. A couple of nights later he took me to a basement apartment in another building. This was not so much to avoid the Germans as to keep neighbouring people from noticing my presence. The reward for my recapture was 1m drachmas — and 1m drachmas would buy food for a family until after the war — even at black market prices! We decided that the basement apartment was fairly safe, but felt sure that undercover men would be posted at strategic points for weeks to come. Before long I got my hands on a self-teaching book on the modern Greek language and began studying. That passed many interminable hours and I knew the knowledge would come in handy when the time came to escape.

He went on to comment on the state of life in Greece in the autumn/winter of 1942, at the time of his escape and evasion:

Twice during the next six weeks we tasted meat: once a can of 'bully beef' that cost 20,000 drachmas, once a delicious piece of pork. I didn't know where it came from and didn't ask .... As for other food — grass tastes like nothing, cooked or raw; carrot tops are bitter; soya beans aren't too bad when one is hungry. Three meals a day were just a heavenly memory. In Greece you spent all your day looking for food, considering it a lucky break if you finished the day with a handful of beans. Being already whittled down to muscle and bone by months of operational service in the desert, I lost only 12lb, and because of inactivity didn't realise how weak I was becoming. I was able to get a fair amount of bread and on average one egg a week. We always had plenty of Greek cigarettes, which I much preferred to English brands.

Matches, salt and bread were the only commodities rationed to the Greek people by the Germans — plenty of matches, not enough salt for health, 60 drams of bread (less than an average slice) per day per person. All other food had to be bought on the black market operated by the Germans and Italians, at unbelievable prices. Many Greeks were forced to work for the invaders, but even they received totally inadequate wages, considering the price of food. A meal with meat from the black market would use up a whole month's salary, leaving one slice of bread a day for the rest of the month. People existed only by selling heirlooms and treasures.

Whatever German brain conceived the plan of keeping a race subjected through physical weakness must have been a brain without blood or tissue, or else had never seen the results. The children on the streets had the pitifully thin arms and distended stomachs that indicated starvation. Many adults looked in the same way, but I was given to understand that conditions had improved.

'Not many will starve this winter', said Bill. 'More wheat is coming from Canada and the US through the International Red Cross, and bread has always been the staple food of these people.'

Occasionally I went out at night to stretch my legs, and was able to see for myself the attitude of the Greek people towards the Italian 'conquerors'. They didn't cringe; they walked the familiar streets with heads held high, never looking directly at, or speaking to, an Italian, ignoring them as if they were mongrel dogs. Many Italians were trying to curry favour through small kindnesses, looking with terror towards the day of an Allied invasion.

Schools were kept open, chiefly to teach the people their new language — German. Church services were allowed, for small numbers of people. When about ten or twelve had entered, the doors were locked; the rest had to wait their turn.

One evening Bill brought in a Luger pistol and handed it over to me. There were five bullets left in it, and I knew that the Hun who'd been carrying it wouldn't be needing it again.

While Hal Marting was still lying low in Athens but was within days of his break-out and the beginning of his evasion, his squadron and those of No 239 Wing were within days of breaking out from El Alamein in the wake of the 8th Army. Meanwhile, the Kitty bombers and the bombers they escorted continued to harry the almost defeated Afrika Korps.

* * * * *

At El Alamein, the great battle was entering its fifth day. On the 28th Miluck noted:

> First show cancelled and nobody complained.[4] Barber and I had an interesting discussion on cold-water-shaving — a serious problem for those with heavy beards: KRs (King's Regulations) require 'a neat appearance at all times'
>
> Plt Off Wright, from 112 Sqn, dropped in to say hello — with a badly bruised head and a black eye. He got a 109 and was watching it crash when flak hit his engine. He managed to stagger over the lines with a cockpit full of glycol fumes, but his seat-straps broke when he crash-landed at 200mph and he got bashed up. Accepting an invitation from him, I had dinner with 112 Sqn and returned home by moonlight, full of beer and rousing cheer.

On 1 November Ed Miluck recorded two operations:

> Judd led 12 aircraft as Kittybombers, bombing west to east along the Gazal Station main road. Enjoyed leading the top six on such a pleasant op, except for the constant nattering of a new pilot who felt bound to report 14 bombers nearby. They were Bostons.

But it was to be a different matter on the second operation:

> In the afternoon Flt Lt Hancock led twelve of us to strafe the Sidi Barrani-Mersa Matruh road. When we had

been up 50 minutes, my fuel pressure dropped to 7lb, indicating the exhaustion of fuel in the belly tank. I switched over to the fuselage tank, twitching a bit at the thought of a petrol shortage if the 'Orrid 'Un' found us. He found us, and I'm still shaking and I'm still scared.

We were on the deck, strafing motor transport, when a standing patrol of Macchi 202s[5] jumped us; nor did anyone see them until Sgt Martin was shot down. There were clouds of smoke from the bombed transport below, which I thought came from Martin's aircraft, and I was bemoaning the loss of a pilot in flames. Thank God somebody saw him belly-land OK.

What an unusual sight — twelve Kittys and four Macchi 202s turning and dodging, skimming the deck, no one ever getting more than 500ft into the air. Now and then one kite would leap above the others like a fish jumping out of water, then fall back and disappear, only to have another kite leap.

In the complete chaos, the Kittys were squirting at each other more than at the 202s, and when the leader told us to turn about there was no need for repetition. Seeing a Kitty quite a distance behind and hearing the radio screech 'Come back, you bastards, come back! What a bunch of bastards!' we made a circle to allow him to catch up. The next thing we saw was a blurred streak as he shot by us; we didn't see him again until we landed. My backside ached after the first hour and the total time was well over two and a half hours. What a shaky do!

No 239 Wing, in its ORB summary of 1 November 1942 operations, did not mention No 250's tangle with the Macchi 202s but concentrated upon No 112's encounter with Ju 87s escorted by Me109s.

197 sorties, comprising armed recces, fighter-bomber and strafing attacks on enemy transport were made throughout the day. When returning from an armed reconnaissance, No 112 Sqn[6] intercepted a formation of 25

to 30 Ju 87s escorted by 15 Me109s, and such was their attack that the Stukas[7] jettisoned their bombs on their own troops. Seven Ju 87s were destroyed, three probably destroyed and five others damaged. One of our pilots is missing from these operations.

Fg Off Miluck made his own, somewhat sardonic, comment on the 1 November operations, noting that

The Eighth Army pushes again tonight and expects armoured clashes and tank battles tomorrow, with armoured cars filtering through gaps in the northern bulge[8] to attack landing grounds. An Army Captain gave us some soft-soap about the superb, magnificent, colossal air support given by the RAF — which was small consolation for the fact that Jerry had scrambled a Macchi squadron to intercept us and had us plotted 30 minutes after we were airborne.

Notes to Chapter 4

1 Quoted in a recent book by the late Vern Haugland, historian of the Eagle Squadrons, called *Caged Eagles Downed American Fighter Pilots 1940–45*, published posthumously by TAB Aero, Blue Ridge Summit, PA 17294-0850.
2 There is no mention of Angela Melidi, nor of her friends Mariette and Litsa, nor of the two sisters Elli and Lilika — all of whom helped Marting and are referred to in the diary he kept in Athens — in his article 'I Escape' in *The American Magazine*. Mariette was in touch with an organization which helped to get escapers/evaders out of Greece, and while the war was still on, any reference which would have implicated her and her brave friends and betrayed them to the Germans had to be avoided.
3 Sqn Ldr J.E.A. Williams DFC commanded No 450 (RAAF) Sqn from October to November 1942. He was succeeded by Sqn Ldr M.C.H. Barber DFC.
4 Miluck was on a 1430–1530hr op — 'escort to bombers, bombing MT and tanks in northern sector'. The No 239 Wing ORB for that day says: 'During Wing escorts to Baltimores and Mitchells bombing enemy MT concentrations five Me109Fs were destroyed and one damaged. We suffered no losses....'
5 Regia Aeronautica monoplane fighter, equivalent to the Hawker Hurricane.
6 Nicknamed the 'shark' squadron because of the 'shark's teeth' insignia painted on the front intakes of their Kittyhawks.
7 Short for *Sturzkampfflugzeug* — 'diving fighter aircraft'.
8 Where an Australian attack towards the sea was followed by Operation 'Supercharge' — the final, successful break-out through the Axis lines — on the night of 1/2 November.

CHAPTER 5
Break-out — from El Alamein and from Athens

Was awakened at 6 am with the news 'We're moving. They're on the run past Fuka!' [wrote Ed Miluck in his diary for 5 November 1942.] Breakfasted on a lime juice and a handful of peanuts, packed my kit and took down our tent. Finished a letter to Mother, the last for some time, I fear. Lost luggage is our chief worry. The only solution seems to be no luggage except what we can carry in our kites. Some of the pilots are packing a bag beneath the seat, one inside the fuselage, three blankets in the bucket seat under the parachute and small articles in each wing. Wrapping-up in three blankets and flopping on the ground to sleep is not too good; I'm taking along the collapsible rubber mattress I bought in Cairo and two slightly tattle-tale grey sheets.

There's still time to do a scheduled patrol between El Daba and Fuka, and a long-range strafe after that, but we're out of petrol. The army is supposed to have armoured cars beyond Mersa Matruh, doing great damage with them — which leaves our morale high. Daba is cleared and we captured nine shiny new Me109s at Gazal Station: 109s are everywhere, crashed or otherwise damaged. But, now comes the word that we must wait till dawn for departure and everyone has to unpack. How we hate this waiting! Dinner tonight will strangely resemble breakfast and lunch — peanuts and beer. But really very filling.

We hear that 4,000 prisoners have been taken. The Greeks sent a pathetic message, 'We have more prisoners than troops. What shall we do?' Yesterday, the Aussies refused to take the Italians who surrendered until barbed wire cages could be provided for them. They told the Italians to 'come back tomorrow' — and they did.

No 239 Wing summed up the operational situation and the beginning of the squadrons' move forward in its ORB entry for 5 November:

> Fighter patrols and bomber escorts were carried out over the Fuka area, and in air combats four Me109Fs were destroyed, one probably destroyed and two damaged. We suffered no losses.
>
> At 1000hr, Wing and Squadron 'A' parties left LG91 for Burg el Arab and were routed from there to LG106. At 1630hr four of our aircraft flew to LG106 and landed. They returned to report that, although the 'A' parties had not yet arrived there, the landing-ground was in serviceable condition. They also reported that in his flight the enemy had left nine Me109s on trucks in Gazal Station.

* * * * *

At almost exactly the same date, Hal Marting began his break-out from confinement in Athens, with the help of his brave friends in the Greek Resistance, as he described it in his account of his evasion:

> At last the time came to make a break. I found out then what we had been waiting for. Bill had acquired a small fishing-boat that the Italians had confiscated, and had hidden it somewhere along the coast. For weeks, gasoline and food bought at black markets had been dribbling through in the hands of friends, an ounce or a gallon at a time, and were stowed away on the boat against future need. Bill thought there was now enough gasoline to get us through to a friendly coast.
>
> In company with some Englishmen and Australians, who had been in Greece since the fighting days[1] and never captured, we set out through the mountains. Every automobile had been taken by the Germans; the only way to get from place to place was on foot.

We had a compass and a map, but in order to keep off the travelled roads we had to climb over some of the roughest country in Greece, and most of Greece is mountainous. We walked 20 or 30 yards apart in single file, each man just keeping the one ahead in view, so that farmers or shepherds working on the lower slopes would not see and remember a group of men.

Bill led the procession. When he threw up his hand, each man behind did likewise and we all dropped down to rest. On the rare occasions when we were close enough to speak, we spoke in whispers, for none of the others knew Greek.

We had no overcoats but wore the odd pieces of clothing we had accumulated. I had on two thin sets of long underwear, two pairs of trousers, two sweaters — one of them sleeveless — and a jacket. There were no buttons on one shabby pair of trousers and I wore them on the outside, overlapping them in front and fastening them together with a safety pin.

As long as we kept on the move we did not suffer from the cold. Each man had a gunny sack[2] containing some food slung over his back. Mine held a big loaf of bread, a tiny square of cheese, a few hard-boiled eggs and some apples. We were able to drink occasionally from mountain streams.

During the middle of each day we hid and rested, travelling early and late and going as long as possible at night to keep warm. And each day the weather seemed colder and the gunny sacks heavier, though they were actually almost empty.

As far as shoes were concerned, I had thought myself much better off than some of the fellows whose shoes were worn down to flimsy wrecks; but my riding boots proved poor friends. They were much too heavy and stiff for walking. By the end of the first day my feet were blistered and sore; by the end of the second they had swelled until they filled the boots completely and there was no longer any pain.

Some of the fellows took off their shoes while we rested; by then, I couldn't have removed my boots if I had wanted to, and after looking at their feet I didn't think I would care to see mine.

* * * * *

On 6 November in the Western Desert there was a new intervention — by the weather. As the official historians[3] described it:

... the skies opened in a deluge which lasted for over twenty-four hours. This hampered Coningham's squadrons and proved still more of a hindrance to Montgomery's armour, which was bogged down as it tried to strike across the desert. Meanwhile, the enemy, moving along the coastal road, gained a flying start ....

No 239 Wing reported on its squadrons' activities on that day, in its Operations Record Book:

Operating from LG91, limited reconnaissances of the road between Mersa Matruh and Sidi Barrani were made. Bad weather prevented good strafing attacks being carried out in this area. From the last operation, the aircraft landed at LG106, now occupied by Wing and Squadron 'A' parties. [This was the beginning of the Wing's moves up the desert in support of the 8th Army.]

Ed Miluck gave a much more picturesque and detailed account in his diary of his activities on that momentous day, which marked the end of the Battle of El Alamein:

Took off before daylight on a reconnaissance flight over enemy airdromes and saw burned transports and tanks making charred black patches on the ground. At least a thousand prisoners were in a close cluster, and huge collections of motor transport and tanks were pushing towards Fuka. No enemy aircraft in the air, but plenty crashed and abandoned on the ground. An exhilarating flight.

4-30 pm. A last, quick scribble before we move up. Have packed my bedding back into the aircraft, with a parachute bag of necessities.

6-00 pm. Arrived at our new landing ground [LG106 — El Daba] and almost wrote myself off twice, due to the rush of pilots trying to get in before dark. No flare paths in this area. Became very annoyed after getting within ten feet of the ground on the second try, so did a very tight circuit at 200ft, 110 mph with wheels and flaps down, and made it that time. The Squadron Leader [Judd] said he could tell it was me landing, by the way I sighed when the wheels touched the ground.

Our new Mess tent has a large red banner with a swastika on the white circle in the centre and a large picture of 'General Field Marshal Rommel'. Looting is well under way. Luger pistols and Leica cameras have already been found, and quantities of rifles, ammunition, water containers and personal articles are everywhere — proof that Jerry pulled out in a hell of a hurry. The amount and range of personal issue equipment astounds us. All of it is far superior to ours; Jerry lacked for nothing. The bloody flies are everywhere, but I ignored them, had a bath in a cup and feel better. And so to bed.

* * * * *

One Wing of the Desert Air Force had thus made its first move in pursuit of the retreating Afrika Korps and *Luftwaffe*; but Hal Marting was beginning to find it hard to move at all:

I began to have a feeling of paralysis from the waist down. It was impossible to swing my legs forward naturally; the only way I could keep going was to take hold of my trouser legs and pull each foot forward like a piece of dead wood. I tried desperately to keep my place in the line, but the ones in front were always having to wait and the ones behind were always catching up, to find me leaning against a rock or a tree. They refused to go on and leave me. By morning I was falling continually on the rocky ground and cutting my face and hands.

At last I lay where I fell. 'Look, you'll have to go on without me.'

It was completely out of the question for them to carry me. Bill said, 'You stay here and rest. I will get some kind of transport and come back for you.'

They helped me down the mountainside and put me in the lee of a big boulder, where I was invisible from the road but could watch for some distance in either direction. The morning sun was warm and bright, and I leaned against the rock and soaked it in numbly. Some distance away a farmer was ploughing his olive grove. Higher up in the hills a shepherd trailed after a lively flock of grazing goats. They saw me, but they made no sign. Some Italians drove past on the road below, their big brown trucks kicking up a cloud of dust. Several times I smoked to keep from dozing.

The next thing that came in sight, about noon, was a man leading a donkey. Not until he turned off the road and started towards me did I recognize Bill. He helped me to get astride the beast, and we travelled the next ten miles along the road itself. At about four o'clock he stopped.

'The village ahead is an Italian garrison town. Can you walk at all?' 'Help me down and we'll see', I said.

I couldn't. The pain was excruciating when I rested my weight on my feet; my knees were like rubber. We looked at each other mutely.

He flung back his streaked hair, looking up the mountain. Then he put an arm around me and half carried me two hundred yards off the road. He spread my empty gunny sack under some low bushes and brought me the blanket from off the donkey.

'Sleep, if you can', he said. 'I'll be back.'

It was dark in a short time, and cold. I pulled the blanket round me as best I could, but it was like nothing between me and the ground. Hour after hour I shivered outwardly and inwardly, my teeth chattering and my stomach shaking, and every twitch reminded me of my feet. It would take weeks for them to heal. Those boots had to come off soon, and when they did ... infection, maybe worse, unless I could find a place to hide where I could get plenty of water to keep them clean, if not some medicine to go on them. But that was an almost hopeless prospect.

Several trucks rumbled by on the road and each time one of them slowed down my heart was in my mouth. The moon came up, inched its way across the sky and faded. The twilight before dawn was an eternity. When the sun came up at last and a little of its warmth began to reach the earth of Greece, I went soundly to sleep ....

* * * * *

With the new day in the Western Desert, the same formula of activity continued — pursuit by the 8th Army of the retreating Afrika Korps, with harassment by the Desert Air Force, which also moved forward to new landing-grounds. No 239 Wing recorded on 7 November its squadrons' departure from the Delta area after the break-out from El Alamein:

At 0700 hours 'B' parties left LG91 [where the Wing had been based since the build-up before the battle] for LG106 [El Daba area] but were later ordered to continue to LG101 [about 80 miles further west]. Patrols and strafing attacks on enemy transport were continued throughout the day from LG106, and in air combat six Ju 52s were destroyed (five of these were carrying petrol) and two Me109s and one Macchi 202 were damaged. We lost three aircraft. On the ground, ten MT vehicles were destroyed and 17 damaged, by strafing.

No 250 Sqn recorded in the early morning (0655 to 0830hr):

> Armed reconnaissance, by six aircraft, of the Barrani road. Columns of MT were strafed along the road, in spite of heavy flak from the road; [then in the afternoon (1500 to 1700hr)]: twelve aircraft took off to strafe the Sollum-Barrani road. They strafed at the 58 Grid easting position, and whilst strafing saw four Ju 52s at deck level flying west. Fg Off Calver, Flt Sgt Chap and Sgt Nitz attacked these and three were shot down in flames; the fourth crashed on landing. Soon after this, Fg Off Troke, Fg Off Calver and Flt Sgt Chap were flying home when they ran into a formation of Ju 87s and fighter escort. Fg Off Troke claims a 109 as probably destroyed. Fg Off Calver was last seen flying underneath the formation. Flt Sgt Chap was attacked by a 109 and seen to crash in flames. Flt Sgt O'Brien also damaged a 109 and Plt Off Russell damaged a Macchi 202.

Ed Miluck had his own adventures on that day — one which showed that the *Luftwaffe* still packed an offensive punch, especially in the hours of darkness:

> First it rained, then the Jerries came over and dropped just enough bombs to keep us awake all night. A scalding hot cup of tea, and we were off on a dawn armed reconnaissance flight to Sollum. Not to disappoint the boys, I led them to some motor transport and we strafed hell out of it all the way home. Tried to sleep after a lunch of vegetable pie and cooked dried peaches, but the flies were too persistent.

He was also on the afternoon sortie, which was nearly his last:

> Scared myself to death on a $2^{1}/_{2}$-hour long-range strafe west of Sidi Barrani. Our first two attacks were down to the deck and resulted in several fires. On the

third strafe, my instruments all went to cock, so I turned south and dived for the deck, expecting the engine to stop at any minute. I had visions of being drawn and quartered by avenging Jerries. The motor kept running, and I had such a good start that I just kept going, flying on the deck all the way home and landing with my emergency undercart gear. 'A few slugs here and there — nothing to worry about', the fitter said casually. Ye Gods!

The others shot down three Ju 52s loaded with petrol, but got separated in the excitement. Plt Off Calver and Flt Sgt Chap formed up with Troke, but had hardly turned for home when they ran into a Stuka party of 20, escorted by 30 109s. Calver either didn't hear, or ignored, Troke's advice not to attack against such odds and was last seen busting into a Stuka with guns blazing. Later, Chap chased a Macchi 202 off Troke's tail, but received some cannon slugs in the cockpit and crashed in flames. Troke got the bastard.

There were three quite different views of the day's operations on 8 November. No 239 Wing noted that 'fighter-bombers and strafing attacks against enemy MT were pressed home during the day's operations, ten MT being destroyed and 25 damaged. We lost one pilot. The 'B' party arrived at LG101'. No 250 Sqn recorded morning and afternoon operations:

0800 to 0945 Six off on sweep, Mersa-Matruh – Charing Cross, which proved uneventful. No enemy aircraft were seen and no flak fired at the formation.

1235 to 1440 Six aircraft as top cover to 112 Squadron bombing in Buq Buq – Sollum area. 112 Squadron bombed a column of MT along the road and all aircraft went down to strafe the road. Approximately ten MT were damaged severely in the attacks. Some light ack-ack was encountered over the target area but no enemy aircraft.

Ed Miluck's diary, however, tells a different story of that day's events:

> Poor 250 Squadron! Six of our pilots are with the other party, God only knows where. 'A' Flight has lost four pilots within forty-eight hours, leaving only five. 'B' Flight has seven pilots. Only ten kites are serviceable. The CO is down with malaria. As a final blow, 'A' Flight commander and two senior pilots, looting in a nearby area, overran a Jerry minefield. Up went a mine, off went a wheel and over went the Jeep. One pilot has broken teeth and severe concussion, another has a broken arm — and, of course, the one who got the idea of looting in the first place escaped except for losing patches of skin.
>
> We have no beer left and no water to make soft drinks. Owing to petrol shortage, each squadron is limited to 18 sorties per day. All our equipment, including the radio, has been sent on to an advanced landing ground. Luckily, Sqn Ldr Barber visited us with the news of US troops landing in North Africa.[4] Tunis, here they come! Everyone is afraid they'll beat us to Tripoli, which would be a dirty trick after all our stooging. I would like a bath.

On 9 November, No 239 Wing and its squadrons moved forward, but continued operating against retreating Axis forces. The Wing HQ, at LG106 at the beginning of the day, recorded that

> during escorts to bombers, fighter-bomber attacks and reconnaissances, one Me 109 was destroyed, two Me 109s probably destroyed, and two Me 109s and one Macchi 202 damaged, for the loss of one of our pilots. 'A' party left LG106 at 0700hr for LG76.

At 0640hr on that day, No 250 Sqn recorded, 'all aircraft took off from LG106 to proceed to LG101'; then in the afternoon, between 1400hr and 1630hr, 'eight aircraft led by Flt Lt Hancock took off on a fighter-bomber attack on the

Sollum road and pass. Immediately after bombing, two Macchi 202s were seen below at approximately 1,000ft. These enemy aircraft were engaged, Plt Off Troke damaging one of them before they made a quick getaway'. Then, later that afternoon (1445hr to 1625hr), 'four aircraft with Fg Off Miluck leading provided a close escort to Bostons bombing the same target as before. Bombing was very accurate on the road. On both occasions today, much heavy flak and some light flak was experienced over the road, especially from the plateau at the top of the pass.'

Ed Miluck himself gave a much more detailed picture of what it was like to move on to another landing ground and at the same time keep up offensive operations. His diary for 9 November records:

> The squadron packed up and pulled out at dawn by truck, leaving ten of us here to bring up the serviceable kite — which we did, arriving at our new base south-east of Matruh [LG101] in 40 minutes' flying time. But where are they? There's nobody here except us chickens. No breakfast, no tents, petrol or ground crews. Four other squadrons have landed in the same condition.
>
> At noon — about the time we were feeling very sorry for ourselves — an Army officer contributed some scrounged tinned food left by the Jerries — peach jam and corned beef with American labels, hard tack, canned tomatoes with an Italian label, cheese, onions, even a can of grapefruit juice. Part of the squadron arrived at last and a few tents went up. A show was scheduled for 1330hr, but in taxying out for take-off, my kite became bogged and neither full throttle nor all the cussing I knew would budge it. Later, was lucky enough to lead the squadron as close cover to 12 Bostons, bombing roads packed with enemy transport.
>
> The Arctic has nothing on us by way of weather tonight, but they say we are here for only 48 hours, then off at our leisure for a new base south of Sidi Barrani. The other Kittyhawk Wing [No 233] should be nearby and in

operations tomorrow. I read last week's paper from cover to cover and feel considerably more optimistic, now that I know what's happening.

This coastal area is very damp and abundant with green camel thorn — abundant, that is, for the desert. It gives off a pleasant sage odour that is soothing when one dozes off in the evening, the dozing hour for me being 7.30. Last thought for the day: the three main functions of a fighter pilot are to eat, to sleep and to kill.

* * * * *

Someone else had dozed off at last — in the warmth of early morning sunshine, lying in the lee of a boulder on a mountainside in Greece, tired of keeping an eye on whatever might be moving on the road below — still a successful evasion or an ignominious recapture? Hal Marting depended entirely on the Greek friend whom he called Bill.

Someone was shaking me and I reached compulsively for the gun. But it was Bill.

'See if you can stand', he said. 'We must catch up with the others.'

I stood up, and kept on standing. I walked a few steps and kept on walking. 'Okay; let's go.'

The village streets were so thick with Italian soldiers that we rubbed shoulders with many of them. We followed the Greek practice of acting as if nothing Italian had ever existed, and evidently the soldiers accepted us as simple civilians, for they let us pass.

A mile or two beyond the village — I had lost all track of distance or time — I stumbled again when the heel came off my boot, and would have fallen if Bill had not been there. My legs were giving out again.

'A little further', he said encouragingly. 'I have a cart ahead.'

We came to a small grove where a donkey was hitched to a two-wheeled wooden cart. Our combined weight in it just about lifted the donkey into the air, but he came back to earth and got going when Bill took up the reins. We rumbled along at a snail's pace until it was dark.

Once Bill stopped close to a farmhouse and went to the door. He came back carrying an old pair of size 12 shoes with soles cut out of tyre treads, which he had bought from the farmer's wife, and also a bundle of bandages and antiseptic.

A few miles further on he lifted his head and sniffed. 'Do you smell the sea?'

I roused myself from my stupor. The air did smell different.

'We must leave the cart here and climb a little more, then we will be there', he said.

That last climb was a nightmare. I simply concentrated on dragging myself ahead one step at a time, and several times I gave up hope completely, but Bill had other ideas. The path would have been hard enough to follow in daylight: at night it was a constant jolting where the ground fell away and a constant stumbling where rocks stood up in our way. At last we crossed the crest and stumbled down the incline to the shore.

After some manoeuvring, Bill located the boat, but the four others in our party were not to be found. It took a silent, three-hour search to locate them inside a shepherd's shelter — a roofless stone wall a few feet high, used as a windbreak.

My boots came off that night. Two of the fellows pulled them off for me, and with them came off the skin of my feet. After the initial pain, this was a relief. I couldn't even feel the antiseptic that was put on them, and when they were bandaged and put into size 12 shoes I found that I could even hobble around a little.

We rested and slept the rest of that night and all of the following day. One of the fellows caught a number of small fish with an improvised seine[5], to conserve our supplies on the boat. We were well hidden, so we built a roaring fire, cooked the fish whole and ate them — scales, bones, tails, heads and eyes. Nothing ever tasted more delicious.

* * * * *

In the desert air war, the Kittyhawk squadrons were now attacking targets on the Egypt–Cyrenaica border. No 239 Wing recorded that 'patrols and reconnaissances were carried out over our armour, with no interference from the enemy. Wing and squadron 'A' parties arrived at LG76'. No 250 Sqn noted that 'twelve aircraft took off on a dawn patrol of the Sollum–Capuzzo area. Two Me109s were seen and attacked but the enemy took successful evasive action and managed to escape. The patrol, apart from this incident, was uneventful. No flak was experienced'. Edward Miluck's own account of the 10 November operation, however, was quite different — recorded with a dry humour:

> A dawn reconnaissance of Fort Capuzzo and area on an empty stomach, observing for the Army, with the flak so heavy and accurate at 5,000ft that we decided to let the Army do its own observation hereafter. Spent an hour and a half blissfully, until I saw two 109s playing behind me. As no one else had reported them, I thought my radio had gone to cock and my weaving went berserk. This poor kite must be getting old; even bending the throttle didn't help my weaving. Such indifference I have never seen. Was chagrined later to find that my radio was working and that I had actually spotted the 109s before anyone else, for a change.
>
> Two new pilots arrived today. Best of all, Sqn Ldr Judd is feeling fit to fly again. I have not seen Wally [Tribken] for some time, but feel sure he can take care of himself. Last rumour about Marting has it that they found his kite intact, with no damage other than that caused by the crash[6].

On 11 November, which Ed Miluck refers to as 'Armistice Day' in his diary, No 239 Wing recorded that 'during fighter sweeps over forward enemy landing grounds and patrols over our forces, five Ju 52s and two Me109Fs were destroyed and one Me109 was damaged. Wing 'B' parties reached LG76 at 1630hr, after leaving LG101 at 0700hr'. Miluck is very much more picturesquely descriptive:

> On the move again. Landed on a cracked-rock runway in a region so barren that it consists of nothing but flat horizon dotted with a few trucks. Impossible to drive tent pegs into the rocky ground, so we are living under a big canvas cover supported by six poles held in place by guys tied to barrels filled with rocks. Reed mats cover the rocky floor except in one corner — which has, by a freak of nature, a six-inch layer of sand. With its open sides, this 'tent' resembles an Arab encampment — air-conditioned, too. Ah, wilderness ... phooey.
>
> What an uncouth group we are — dirty beards, matted hair, grease-stained shirts and trousers. Fatigue is evident everywhere. Two or three Lockheeds are always on the horizon, landing or taking off, supplying us with petrol and water[7], but we still receive only two pints of water per day — hardly enough to drink; no washes, no shaves. Back at El Alamein, we lived like kings. I even remember giving some water away.
>
> Jerry still holds Sidi Barrani, Sollum, Halfaya and Bardia, but we are working parallel to the coast to by-pass him and get to Tobruk. Sweeps are going on constantly. Twelve of our aircraft started for a show over Tobruk but only ten got away. The rocks are so sharp that three kites have already burst tail-wheel tyres. One of the kites, returning early, just landed and flipped on to its back with its wheels sticking up towards the sky — one of the strangest sights I have seen: the pilot is OK. No 2 (SAAF) Sqn jumped 15 Ju 87s this afternoon, destroyed eight and got four probables. 65 USAAF Sqn pursued and destroyed three Stukas landing at their base[8].
>
> Shocked by the horrible sight of three Kittyhawks going up in flames, due to a take-off collision. One pilot

— 'Tex' Phillips of No 112 Sqn — badly burned, which means months in a hospital. These narrow runways are a hazard. Amazing, the way all-metal aircraft burn so fiercely, with such intense heat and such clouds of smoke. A fourth kite had to belly-land after damaging his undercarriage when he hit an oil drum.

My faith in Wally's ability to take care of himself is shaken. An exploding petrol can sprayed burning fuel over his face, head and back. He was rushed to Cairo, bemoaning his carelessness, and they say he will be all right after three weeks in hospital.

Gambut, south-east of Tobruk, was now the objective of the No 239 Wing squadrons, which continued operating while their bases moved forward. Thus the Wing's Operations Record Book recorded on 12 November:

Fighter sweeps were made over the Tobruk and Gazala areas during the day, with little opposition from enemy aircraft. 'B' party left LG76 at 0500hr, and arrived [at] Gambut satellite No 1 at 1630hr.

Then on the following day the move forward was completed: 'No operations. 'A' party left LG76 for Gambut'.

Ed Miluck saw the start of this move from the air. In his diary for the 12th he wrote:

Did a brief solo at dawn and watched our advance party trail off toward Gambut with their numerous trucks. Four new pilots have arrived. When one of them asked where the water fountain was, we told him to go out to the slipstream and get a bucket of propwash.

On the 13th, the move was completed:

The squadron packed up and moved on at dawn, the remaining trucks following at 8 am. Because of haze and mist, we couldn't follow with the kites until noon. Lunch consisted of a can of bully beef and some dry biscuits eaten in the shade of the planes. Not a thing in sight in the whole damned wilderness except 14 aircraft.

Had a hell of a landing at Gambut, due to excess weight of blankets, kit, belly tank and a very hazy horizon. One pilot crashed. It was my misfortune to be on readiness from 3 pm until sundown, breathing in pounds of dust. This is the worst 'drome for dust in the desert, they say. The other Kitty Wing [No 233], a Spitfire Wing and a Hurricane Wing are nearby. Tobruk fell today and the Army gives us a new advance bomb-line every few hours ... whizzo! Everyone had their tents up by dusk except us 'readiness boys'. We pitched ours in the dark, only to have it collapse in the middle of the night.

The Official Historians thus summed up this astonishing progress, since the break-out from El Alamein:

For weeks which stretched into months the pursuit across Libya rolled on. By 13th November the Eighth Army was in Tobruk and the Western Desert Air Force at Gambut.[9]

Notes to Chapter 5

1   Which ended in May 1941 when the Allied forces were evacuated.
2   Coarse sacking. A 'gunny' is a sack, usually of jute fibre (OED).
3   *Royal Air Force 1939–1945 Vol II The Fight Avails*, by Denis Richards and Hilary St George Saunders (HMSO).
4   Operation Torch, which began on 8 November 1942.
5   OED defines as 'fishing net for encircling, with floats at top and weights at bottom edge'.
6   Marting's had been a good forced-landing: he was presumed to have been taken PoW.
7   Lockheed Hudsons and Douglas Dakotas of Nos 117, 173, 216 and 267 Sqns flew up fuel, water and ammunition to the Desert Air Force squadrons.
8   The DAF was an Allied Air Force, with USAAF squadrons involved in the El Alamein battle and the final advance to Tunis.
9   *Royal Air Force 1939–1945 Vol II The Fight Avails*, by Denis Richards and Hilary St George Saunders (HMSO).

Pilots collected from their aircraft after a sortie. The squadron letters are on the door of the truck. Ed Miluck is standing up with his hands on his hips.

Fg Off Miluck contemplating his cockpit — after he had received an explosive shell in it. The lock of the Sutton harness can just be seen over the side.

Refuelling by bowser at LG91. The groundcrew — who refuelled, rearmed and maintained the aircraft — were the mainstay of every squadron.

Captured Junkers Ju 87 Stuka 'under new management'.

CHAPTER 6
Across the Sea to Freedom

Hal Marting and his fellow evaders were still in Greece, on the edge of the Aegean Sea, scene of so many classical adventures — from the days of Troy and Ulysses onwards. They had been provided with the means of escape by their brave Greek friends, but had no idea what lay ahead for them on those 'wine-dark waters':

The boat was about 25ft long, equipped with sails and a little one-cylinder auxiliary engine. It had a hold about four by six feet in size, with a tarpaulin cover designed to keep the sun from spoiling the fish. This was to be our hiding place. Bill, of course, was to be the 'fisherman', and he gave strict orders that not more than one of us at a time was to appear on deck. One extra person would pass as a helper. There was food enough to last for two days and plenty of fresh water.

At 8 o'clock in the evening we cranked up the engine and pulled away from the Grecian shore, planning to cross the most dangerous stretch of water near the coast under cover of darkness. As soon as we left the sheltered cove and pulled into open water we were at the mercy of German and Italian patrol boats — and we knew that the coast was patrolled constantly. The five of us lay flat on the deck near the hold, watching the thin silhouette that was Bill at the stern, straining our eyes and ears into the surrounding blackness; but there was no sound — except for the slap of the waves and the chug-chug of our engine.

Before dawn we crawled one by one into the stinking hold, and for the next 17 hours lay stretched out full length, side by side, so that there would be enough room for us all. Many small islands dotted the sea in that region and a few other fishing craft were out, Bill reported; but if he saw a patrol boat he never mentioned it.

The first time I was allowed up on deck to exercise my legs, I pulled out the Luger that had been my last hope against recapture.

'I'm going to shoot this thing', I called by way of warning, and pulled the trigger. *Click, click, click, click.* The gun misfired four times before a bullet finally splashed into the water.

Toward dark, we heard a shout from Bill. He was pointing ahead, where far in the distance lay a hazy mound of something that might easily be cloud: but it was land. Bill altered course and headed directly for it, the engine chugging hopefully. I noticed the other fellows glancing back over their shoulders, scanning the water intently for anything as small as a periscope. I felt the same way. Land was still far ahead. About two miles from it, the engine began to splutter — but it got us there. We would have paddled in with our hands if necessary.

It was a small port with a pier Bill was heading for, and beyond it we could see the spires of a city. A crowd of curious natives were there to see what riff-raff the tide had brought them this time, and they watched our slow and painful disembarkation. We sent one of them off to notify British authorities of our arrival.

No one who has not been hunted like a wild animal for months could quite understand our feelings as we stood there on free soil. We were ragged, unshaven and filthy; all of us had bad feet and some of us could hardly stand: but we were free men, and there was a big grin on every face.

These escapers/evaders were at last among friends; but Marting's original helper, and the man who led them to safety — whom they only knew as Bill, just disappeared.

We were given the best of care and the finest foods — real coffee with cream and sugar, steaks, chicken, fresh fruits, chocolate bars, clean sheets, clean clothes, baths and beer.

'Is there anything else you want?' asked a nurse who stopped by my bed.

'Yes, please', I said. 'Ice cream'.

We rested five days, but on the third I was up and around in a huge pair of felt bedroom slippers which I tied on with strings. One of the Greek shoes had almost lost its sole; it was ripped from the back half-way to the toe, so that my bandaged heel kept coming down on the ground. I climbed out of bed and went to see how the others were doing.

'Where's Bill?' I asked when I had looked them over.

'He left this for you', said one of them, handing me a leather cigarette case.

Bill hadn't waited for thanks. I felt pretty bad at first, but I guess it wasn't really necessary. Wherever he is, he knows.

In Western Turkey, Hal Marting and his fellow ex-PoWs were still a long, long way from Cairo. As he put it in his article for *The American Magazine*:

The next question was getting back to Egypt. Civilians were not allowed to pass the border without visas, which would have taken months to obtain, but there was a standing arrangement for troops to pass. We were given temporary passports and put into Australian Army privates' uniforms, but I had to stick to my bedroom slippers because my feet were not yet in condition for shoes.

Before the start of their journey, he had bought a 1943 Turkish pocket diary — it was now only a week before Christmas 1942; and in this he recorded their progress in firm, clear handwriting, at first in pencil and then in ink.

CHAPTER 7
The Advance Westwards

During the long, painful weeks when Hal Marting had evaded recapture, Ed Miluck had gone forward with No 250 Squadron of No 239 Wing, Desert Air Force — flying Kittyhawk fighter-bomber sorties in support of the advancing 8th Army and enduring all the discomforts and privations of moving from one hastily-prepared landing-ground to another, recently evacuated by the *Luftwaffe*. So swift was the advance that ground parties were pushing on again after only a few hours, while the squadrons were operating. On 14 November, at Gambut No 1, No 239 Wing recorded in its ORB:

> Several fighter-bomber attacks on enemy transport. Wing and Squadron 'A' parties arrived Gambut 1145hr, leaving again for Gazala No 2 at 1300hr. Arrived Gazala 1730hr.

At Gazala No 2, on the 15th,

> long-range sweeps were made over the Derna, Barce and Benghazi areas, one He111 being shot down. 'B' party reached Gazala from Gambut at 1700hr.

But on the 16th they were on the move again, with operations still going on:

> Patrols were carried out over the Barce–Tocra area, and one Me109 was destroyed. At 0800hr, Wing and Squadron 'B' parties left Gazala for Martuba.

Ed Miluck found some comfort, while at Gambut, in being within reach of the sea — though there were not many other compensations. He wrote on the morning of 14 November:

Refreshed again after twelve hours' sleep, I wonder if a normal bed will ever feel the same again. I do not sleep as well either in Cairo or in Alexandria as in the desert.

Some day I will write an ode to canned corned beef. If it was good, I wouldn't like it. A cheese-pickle paste almost disguises the taste, but not quite. Breakfasted on beans and you-know-what, but a can of honey scrounged by Holmes helped sweeten the day for me, thank God. Yesterday was my ill-humour day and I made an ass of myself.

We are ten miles from the coast — almost two hours of dusty driving, but some of us managed to get there. A warm, relaxing swim in the Mediterranean, with powdery white sand for a mud pack, made us tingle and glow. The odour permeating our close quarters was getting a bit high.

But this was a brief respite from operations and the relentless move forward:

Stooged on another sweep of the Mekeila area. No motor transport or enemy aircraft in sight, though we are amazed at the large number of crashed and burned Stukas — dozens of them — lying about the landing-grounds. I felt so good I did rolls and sundry aerobatics all the way home. The *Luftwaffe* is supposed to have withdrawn as far as Benghazi, so we leave for Gazala in the morning.

The squadron was released at 3 pm and the pilots are amusing themselves with a box of Jerry 'Very' shells[1], as delighted as children: it looks like the Fourth of July. Food being our prime concern, today has been a red letter day, starting with a pre-lunch snack of tongue and biscuits garnished by pears. At tea time Freddie, the cook, slipped me a plate of spaghetti — but Collier caught us in the act and I had to share the loot. Managed to compromise and combine it with a can of his tomato soup. Excellent!

Ed Miluck had the unique experience of making the next move on four wheels instead of by air, seeing many things he would not otherwise have seen and being bombed en route:

We left Gambut at 8 am and unpacked at Gazala at noon, which shows what tarmac roads can do. For the first time, I travelled by road, driving the commanding officer's car. Nor did I envy the pilots: they had no sooner landed and refuelled than off they went on a hell of a long reconnaissance of Benghazi.

Our drive was pleasant until we approached Tobruk and stopped to investigate the dozens of wrecks on two abandoned airfields within walking distance of the town. Had just pulled off the road when in from the sea came three bombers at about 15,000ft. As we stared, the drone of their engines became near and horrible — the weird sound of Junkers Ju 88s. We scattered frantically as they bombed the road, then cheered like hell when one of them went straight down and crashed in a cloud of smoke. One moment it was standing on its nose in the air, the next it had crumpled into the ground. No one baled out. A complete mystery, as there was no ack-ack and none of our aircraft around. Earlier this morning, 109s had strafed the same road with more success. 'Home is the sailor, home from the sea, and the hunter home from the hill...'.

Pitiful Tobruk is nothing but a crumpled pile of rubble and shattered buildings, surrounding a harbour full of half-submerged, derelict ships. For all its fame in this war, it is still a mere Arab village, cowering under the drone of aircraft.

Arriving at Gazala, I tore into a can of sardines, not waiting for lunch thirty minutes later. It consisted of bullybeef, fried onions and beans, which I also ate. Best of all, the mobile canteen arrived and I ate a whole can of honey-sweet peaches.

Heavy air activity keeps the loose dirt continually stirred up, obliterating everything except for the sky directly overhead. A show scheduled for Benghazi petered out because of dust clouds, which was OK, as most of the aircraft need inspection and check-ups. Spare parts are out of the question. We need rest and reorganization before getting within range of those retreating 109s with their backs to the wall.

Paddy Cairns, flying forward from our last airfield, had to force-land and was picked up by our slow-moving ground convoy. He said, 'One minute the engine was purring along beautifully, the next it was a hunk of hot metal.' Twenty-year-old Paddy is the veteran of the squadron in desert warfare, having had more than a year of it with 250 alone. He has advanced this far several times before, but with a bit of persuasion admits that we *might* get through this time.

Water, water everywhere — and not a drop to drink, so everyone is bathing and shaving instead. I washed my hair, which changed my appearance so materially that there was no end of comment — mostly lewd. Discussing beards, one Aussie pilot said, 'We jokers know we can grow one; you buggers have to show one to prove it.' I wonder if anyone will understand my language when I get home? — if I ever get home. So far today, one aircraft has had to force-land and three have crashed on landing: we take off around, in front of, behind and between them.

This place is beyond description in filth and dust: any resemblance to an aerodrome is purely coincidental. Our new Mess is an underground cavern, with seven steps winding down to an irregularly-shaped room about 20ft long by 12ft wide. The pilots are seated under a hole in the roof, reading or listening to the radio; but by the time dinner is finished at 5 o'clock it will be dark and bedtime will be upon us. An adjoining room, which lacks the air hole in the ceiling and is therefore less popular, contains a table and six chairs — pushed around just as Jerry left them.

On the 16th the weather intervened and there was tragedy on the squadron:

> A steady drizzle since midnight hampers flying, but the 500ft cloud base, which has gone up and down like a stage curtain on a busy night, is lifting quite a bit now. Sqn Ldr Terry, Sqn Ldr Strausan and several airmen were blown up by a land-mine this morning — the mine showing its usual disregard for rank. One of the older (in experience) pilots is leaving as a result of his crash yesterday. His previous crack-up was entirely his fault and this second one settled the matter. Drastic treatment, but necessary, with aircraft being so valuable.
>
> Had an excellent afternoon scrounging cheese, onions, margarine, biscuits and beer. Borrowed a Primus stove from the Mess and a frying-pan for the onions. Added them to a can of cheese that had been melting on the Primus and mixed a delectable golden paste to spread on the biscuits. A pinch of salt and a can of beer finished it off.
>
> The weather has cleared and the sun shines furtively from behind the clouds, as if it dreaded to see what would happen next down below. I hope the rumour that we will spend the next ten days at Martuba doing detestable convoy patrols is merely talk. My guess is that Jerry won't make a stand, but will use the Tunisian airfields as a rear guard while his army in Libya pulls off a Dunkirk. Anyway, the Eighth Army plans to consolidate its gains for three days before continuing, which is what we wanted in the first place.

Benghazi, with at least five airfields in its vicinity, presented a big target for the Kittyhawk fighter-bombers, No 239 Wing recording on 17 November that

> Successful fighter sweeps over Benghazi and Magrun were made during the day, and in the air six He111s, two Me109Fs and one Ju 52 were destroyed.... On the ground,

three He111s and two SM84s, one SM79, one Me110, one Ju 52 and ten MT vehicles were destroyed and one Ju 52, two Breda Posts and 36 MT vehicles (some troop-carrying) were damaged. Three of our pilots are missing. By destroying seven enemy aircraft in the air, No 250 Squadron brought their total destroyed to over 100.

Ed Miluck had his own, more detailed account of this day's operations:

> After sitting in our kites from dawn until 9 o'clock, waiting for the rain to let up, I led six aircraft on a two-hour show, but had to turn back because of bad weather over the target — bags of low stratus cloud rolling over the ground for miles.
>
> In the afternoon, the weather broke and a second detail of 12 aircraft repeated the show and really hit the jackpot. I'm almost too miserable to write about it. They went to Benina airfield, near Benghazi, caught six Heinkel 111s in the act of landing, and Hancock, Taylor and Troke each set one on fire with their first bursts. Plinston pursued and destroyed a petrol-carrying Ju 52, last seen crashing and setting a hangar alight. Stewart attacked a Heinkel on the deck, and although hit by the rear gunner's bullets, pressed home his attack and destroyed the aircraft, while Nitz nimbly chased another one in and out of the clouds for several minutes before hitting one of its engines and setting it on fire. Still another one fell to Holmes.
>
> Not satisfied, the boys proceeded to strafe the dozens of 'planes dispersed wingtip to wingtip on the aerodrome for refuelling. Nitz and Plinston left three burning in one fire. Taylor destroyed a Ju 52 on the ground. Hancock, the leading scorer, set a Heinkel and two SM82s on fire, making his total for the day two in the air and three on the ground, all flamers. Newton was ashamed to admit that he had shot down only one aircraft, a SM79. What a lucky bunch of bastards!

Word comes that the pilots' claims were modest. At least another score of aircraft were destroyed or damaged by spraying petrol and explosions. The airfield was left a blazing inferno. The roads around it were jammed with enemy transport and all stopped to watch the slaughter. One pilot flew so low he could see the Jerry troops shaking their fists. Many of them made futile attacks with pistols and rifles, but no serious ack-ack was encountered. The whole show took less than seven minutes.

To celebrate, the corporal in charge of messing laid a sumptuous table and ever-dear liquor appeared like magic. The padre arrived with a water can full of Chianti wine, which was drunk by all, including a not-too-sober padre. Wing Commander Haysom and the boys also drank to the squadron's victories, now numbering over 100.

No 250 Squadron's 'century' had thus been duly recorded by its own private diarist, who on 18 November elaborated its ORB note of 'offensive sweeps of Benghazi, Benina, Msus and Magrun areas' with his own more detailed and personalized account:

Feeling better this morning after an aerial Cook's Tour of Benghazi, Benina, Msus, Barce, Apollonia, Derna and Martuba. We strafed Benina aerodrome again and destroyed six more aircraft on the ground. Also made a dawn reconnaissance of Barce, but again had to return due to bad weather — rain and clouds down to the deck.

After flying between deep valleys of white cloud without being able to see the ground below or the sun above, we suddenly burst out into soft sunshine. I felt as if I were flying from heaven to earth through a huge cathedral with a great blue dome. The sun's rays slanted down in bright rainbow colours, as if they had passed through stained-glass windows.

For a pleasant interval, we rested our desert-weary eyes on green patches of vegetation far down below. Gentle green hills, criss-crossed with brown stripes of roads and dotted with white cottages, gave the area almost an air of agricultural prosperity. But the Army is racing to the south to cut off the remnants of Rommel's armoured divisions at Benghazi — about 40 tanks without petrol and 15,000 troops. They expect a Dunkirk if they can keep him from getting through El Agheila pass — only five miles wide and impassable on either side.

For the first time, I saw six Flying Fortresses. Beautiful monsters!

We have been doing convoy patrols all day and should be relieved by Malta Spitfires tomorrow. Supplies for that tiny island — down to only nine days rations of food and petrol — are being rushed in by destroyers and cruisers.[2]

On 19 November the No 239 Wing squadrons moved westwards again — to Martuba. It took the convoy carrying all the equipment six and a quarter hours (1445 to 2100hr), but Ed Miluck did it in considerably less time:

A windy, gusty day with bags of dust. Covered the road trip to our new base (65 miles) in four hours, and by reckless driving through minefields arrived in time for a hot dinner. Got our beds made before dark. My shivering bones were warmed considerably by a double rum issued by the doc. The cold, damp air is unbelievably penetrating. What wouldn't I give for a hot bath, a warm bed and a blonde de-icer.

On the 20th he was flying again from the new landing-ground, Martuba No 4, when as No 239 Wing recorded: 'patrols were made over our forward troops in the Msus–Agedabia areas, and reconnaissance flights were made as far as El Agheila without encountering opposition.

The pilots' view was different, however, as he noted in his diary:

Led top cover on a dawn armed reconnaissance over the Msus, Antelat and Agedabia areas. The Army said yesterday that we had taken these points and would somebody please fly over to make sure. Over we went at 5,000ft and got everything thrown at us but the kitchen sink. We pulled out in a hell of a hurry and were still cussing the Army when we landed.

The No 250 Sqn ORB confirmed Ed Miluck's description of this operation — which, though he did not know it then, was to be his last with the squadron. The ORB compiler[3] recorded that ten Kittyhawks led by Sqn Ldr Judd

...carried out a sweep over Agedabia to cover our forward troops. Before taking off they were informed that the Agedabia landing-ground was occupied by our forces but on arriving there were greeted by bursts of 88mm flak from six guns located in the southern dispersal. This caused them to make a hurried getaway from the vicinity of the landing-ground. No enemy aircraft were seen on the landing-ground and none were encountered in the air. Squadron returned after a 2hr 10min round trip.

Ed Miluck also noted in his diary entry for 20 November:

A Stuka is being used to bring mail and beer from Alexandria. Surprising, how much beer a Stuka will carry.[4] The cold forces us to wear long-sleeved shirts and turtle-neck sweaters in addition to our heavy — and supposedly warm — battledress. Even the idea of wearing battledress seemed an impossibility in Cairo, but now the sun is a rare treat and we see less and less of it the further west we travel. And I left England because it was cold and damp! But this meets with much approval from the British members of the squadron — 'actually, just like jolly old England, old boy'.

Benghazi fell today, but with only 700 prisoners. What happened to the 15,000?

On 21 November, when 'only three sorties were made during the day' (in the words of the No 239 Wing ORB), Ed Miluck — who 'slept late and did nothing until after lunch, the weather being very bad' — noted in his diary a friendly visitor and some unfriendly ones:

> Sqn Ldr Clouse of No 601 (Spitfire) Sqn dropped in, flying his private Stuka. At least three Ju 88s were hovering in the clouds at 10,000ft and they bombed us twice, once on the road and once on the landing-ground proper, but with very little damage.

He did his last flying with No 250 (Sudan) Sqn on the 22nd — an air test of Kittyhawk FR332.

During the latter part of November, very few operations were carried out by the No 239 Wing squadrons, owing to the distance between the Wing and the enemy lines. As Ed Miluck put it in his diary entry for 25 November: 'The bomb line is now past Agedabia, which is two and a half hours' flying time away — our maximum range. We are on one hour's notice.

It was perhaps just as well for No 250 Sqn that from 22 to 30 November there were practically no operations — for, as Miluck noted:

> 'Illness is rampant. Sqn Ldr Judd, with yellow jaundice, is being sent to a Cairo hospital. Hancock is ill with abdominal trouble. The rest of us have to queue up at the desert lily'. He himself had, on the 22nd, 'finally succumbed to doc's wishes and gulped some foul medicine to counteract a three-day attack of Gyppo-gut, otherwise known as Malta Waltz. No matter what you call it, it still means numerous frantic dashes at most inconvenient hours to the outdoor lavatory, which is uncomfortable in the daytime and hell in the middle of a wet night'.

During November, No 239 Wing had advanced a distance of nearly 550 miles and its squadrons had continued to operate, their pilots backed up by the energy and keenness of the ground staffs. But it is not surprising that the strain of operations, the dust and flies, primitive living conditions and a monotonous diet had taken their physical toll of all personnel.

There was to be another move at the end of November–beginning of December, from Martuba to Antelat, and from 26 November to 7 December the Wing was released from operations — its pilots being granted five days' leave.

For Ed Miluck, this break could not have come at a more appropriate time. He had noted on 27 November: 'Doc has taken me off flying for 48 hours'; then on the 30th:

> Couldn't sleep a wink last night. Very unwell and too sick to eat any breakfast, but managed to pack my kit and bedroll, as it is now my turn for five-day leave. Shivered for hours in a cold drizzle, waiting for the Bombay[5] to pick us up. And now we leave this romantic land of the ever-shifting sands and turn our eyes toward that mysterious Mecca, Cairo.[6]

Notes to Chapter 7

1   Flares fired from a signal pistol, for recognition or distress, named after S.W. Very, who invented the system.
2   Despite being beleaguered and suffering acute shortages and discomforts, Malta played a decisive role in the desert war by intercepting Rommel's supply convoys — identified by reconnaissance aircraft, then attacked by Royal Navy submarines and torpedo-carrying Fleet Air Arm Albacores and RAF Beauforts.
3   Tribute should be paid here to the compilers of the Operations Record Books — handwritten in the cases of No 239 Wing and No 250 (Sudan) Sqn — who daily recorded their operations as they advanced from landing-ground to landing-ground in support of the 8th Army. These ORBs are now kept in the Public Record Office.
4   The Junkers Ju 87 Stuka dive-bomber, which had earned itself a terrifying reputation in France in 1940, was a big single-engined aircraft — normally carrying a two-man crew, 12ft 9^1/$_2$in high and 37ft 8^1/$_2$in long with a 45ft 3^1/$_2$in wingspan.
5   Bristol Bombay, a high-winged monoplane with a fixed undercarriage, designed as a bomber but used in the Middle East for transport duties.
6   On 28 November he wrote in his diary: 'A visiting Hurricane pilot says that Bob Mannix bought it while ground strafing. I hope he is wrong. Bob came with us from the Eagle squadron and only a few weeks ago became a Squadron Leader, CO of No 33 Sqn (Hurricanes), which is damned good for a Yank in the RAF.... I wonder if Wally knows about Bob'.

Army-Air Force co-operation: the RAF refuels some tanks and scout cars near Sidi Barrani.

Back to the desert — by Bristol Bombay of No 216 Sqn.

Fg Off Falconer-Taylor (right), who 'walked casually into the Mess' on 26 October after force-landing in enemy-held territory and walking for more than 90 miles with a broken hand.

No 250 Sqn ready to move in the advance westwards: the telephone line is the last piece of equipment to be packed up.

CHAPTER 8
A Cairo Interlude

The threat of war — of invasion by the Afrika Korps, of air raids and of military occupation by the Axis Powers — had long since receded from Egypt. The 8th Army was now well past Benghazi and its next triumph would be the recapture of Tripoli. The ancient city of Cairo had returned to its normal state — a centre of high-level military command, of diplomatic policy-making and intrigue, of social life interrupted for a time by the scare of the enemy being at El Alamein, of great wealth coexisting with squalid poverty and overcrowding, of teeming millions trying to make a living or just to eke out an existence, of colour, unceasing movement, dirt and noise.

Ed Miluck knew exactly what he wanted when he got there — most men did, when they got back from 'the blue', and Cairo could always provide it, whatever it was — and spent his first day's leave in leisurely style:

> Breakfasted on bacon and genuine omelette — my first taste of eggs in a month. Back to bed until noon, when Wally [Tribken] returned with some campho-phenique to chase away the mobile dandruff collected in the desert. He emerged from the hospital without scars.
>
> Spent the afternoon loafing and eating, and when that became monotonous, switched to eating and loafing. Had my fourth soapy shower before tearing into a dinner of steak and wine. While the others enjoyed American cigarettes, I drowsily contemplated the delights of a comfortable bed with a real mattress and clean sheets, then turned over and went to sleep.

He had keen eyes for the everyday aspects of Cairo life, for on his second day there (2 December) he noted in his diary:

> During an hour's walk, these sights impressed me: A grubby child crying silently because she fell and dropped

the piece of meat she was eating, which a dog snatched up. A group of musicians with puffed cheeks and strained faces, making weird music. A smooth-faced young man performing an Egyptian snake dance, the fanatical gleam in his black eyes indicating that he was slightly hopped.[1] A shifty, one-eyed beggar shuffling from eating shop to eating shop, begging a piece of greasy meat which he gulped down like a dog. Cinema advertisements in Arabic, with James Cagney, Ann Sheridan and Pat O'Brien depicted with Egyptian facial characteristics — black-rimmed eyelids, slanting eyes, swarthy complexions and copious moles. If these actors knew how much weight they had put on, it would worry them no end.

A basket-weaver in full production on a street corner, his tools being a pair of agile hands and sharp teeth for cutting the stout cords. Numbers of men entering and leaving a Mosque, each removing his shoes before climbing the carpeted stairs and each carrying them in the same way — heel to heel and sole to sole. There must be some significance in this. A funeral procession disappearing down a side street, composed of men only — as usual, in black gowns and bright aprons, with a solitary musician playing a reed instrument beside the inevitable, unwieldy casket. In the slummier quarters, each narrow, winding alley has its quota of goats, dogs and sleeping humans sprawled across the pathways — figures whom everyone steps over, but does not disturb. If privacy is sought, the sleeper wraps a cloth around his face.

All Servicemen set out to find something in Cairo to send home, discovering the pleasures and pitfalls of such an expedition. On 3 December, Ed Miluck noted:

Went shopping in the bazaars, buying gifts for relatives and friends — hand-made silver bracelets, tarbushes, perfumes, spices and a few leather articles. The traders believe in charging what the traffic will bear and they haven't had to study economics to learn how. There is no such thing as a fixed price: the higher your rank, the more expensive the article. From British Tommy to RAF airman, to British Army officer to RAF officer, to American soldier to American officer, the prices skyrocket. There are also subtle differences between men of the same rank and nationality: an aircrew officer can afford to pay more than a non-flying officer.

There is a gap in Ed Miluck's Cairo diary for 4 December, and his entry for the 5th attempts to explain why:

As I sit in bed, contemplatively scratching myself, I look back in amazement on the happenings of yesterday and last night. Bix and Mac[2] dropped in at 10 am and we celebrated their transfer to the USAAF with a few cans of beer. Wally and three Fleet Air Arm pilots rendered a musical sonata on reed flutes and by noon a score of people were boisterously enjoying themselves in our hotel room. Everyone was arguing with two US Army privates professing to be FBI men. Sometime during the night, I deposited several queer types in the hall, managed to lock the door and get to bed. Now that I think about it, I didn't leave the hotel once yesterday. In fact, I never got past the pyjama stage of dress or undress.

That day, 5 December, was their last day's leave in Cairo and they celebrated accordingly, as Miluck recorded on the 6th:

They tell us we had a damned good time last night. After visiting Groppi's, Doll's Cabaret and the Kursaal, we started for the hotel by horse and gharry, loaded with beer, chickens, bolognas[3], sausages, cheeses, salads, bread and pickles, but no tableware or plates. Max played host and gallantly ripped the chickens in half with his bare, almost clean hands, giving everyone a half chicken and a benevolent, spine-jarring slap on the back with the admonitions 'Eat! Drink!' It seems that Wally won a gharry race at 4 am on one of the wider streets. Max's team came in second and a friend of his third, while I stood and consoled the gharry drivers with a big, empty .45 automatic.

Despite the ordeals of 'the night before', they were ready on the 6th to go back to the Desert Air Force:

Wally and I left Almaza Airport, Cairo, to return to the squadron at Martuba, making the flight in a tired old Bombay that never got more than 200ft off the ground during the $3^1/_4$-hour trip. It's a wonder it ever got off the ground. There were 23 of us beside the crew, each carrying a case of beer in addition to regular baggage. Stopped at Mersa Matruh long enough to see the boys in No 127 Squadron, but they were mostly on leave and I couldn't find out any more about Bob Mannix. Looks kind of bad, and that has taken a lot out of us.

Arrived at muddy Martuba and retired to a soaked bed.

Notes to Chapter 8

1 Under the influence of drugs.
2 Bix was Edwin Bicksler, who after being transferred to the USAAF served with one of its fighter squadrons in the Desert Air Force and was shot down in Tunisia in April 1943. It has not proved possible to identify Mac.
3 Bologna was a seasoned smoked sausage of beef, pork and veal.

'On the move' between landing-grounds — a lunch of sardines.

Downed enemy — a Macchi 200.

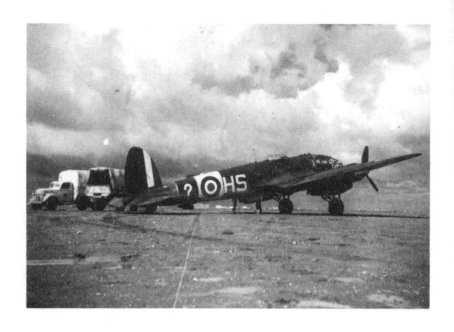

Liquid transportation: ex-Luftwaffe He III bringing in beer and an RAF Dakota bringing in petrol.

CHAPTER 9
Back to the Desert Air War

No 239 Wing ORB recorded the weather which accounted for the 'muddy Martuba' to which Ed Miluck returned: 'Considerable heavy rain fell on 4th and 5th December and much of the camp was flooded.' But they were not to be there for much longer: 'On 6th December, 'A' party moved from Antelat to Belandah Landing Ground No 1'; and, on the 8th: 'All aircraft flew from Martuba No 4 to Belandah No 1, and, from there, one escort to Tac R Hurricanes on reconnaissance of Marsa Brega and El Agheila was carried out. 'B' party left Martuba for Belandah.'

Ed Miluck just had time to record one domestic detail, for on 7 December he noted:

> We have a pet goat now, named Julius — a little black kid that gets thoroughly beaten up by our cat, Stuka. Like all women, she hates to see anyone take her place in our affections.

But on the 9th he too was involved in the move to Belandah:

> Busy packing for another advance. I never seem to have enough room for all the loot I accumulate: this time I have to leave a couple of good Hun helmets. I'm doing all the driving, as the four other pilots are English and don't know how. The country gets prettier all the time — looks a lot like California except that many Roman ruins can be seen. We are out of the desert and in a civilized country, but there is much pitiful evidence of the people we have dispossessed.[1]

On the second day of their journey he recorded enemy air activity:

Since 2 am a couple of Huns have been over us, keeping the place alight with flares and incendiaries. Little damage, but it's the first time we've been bombed in a month and we're out of practice.

On the road again after breakfast, averaging 40mph all the way to Benghazi, which without exception is the most wrecked town I have ever seen. Everything not hit by bombs or shell-fire was destroyed by the retreating Hun. In the railway station are a couple of forlorn, burned-out trains waiting for passengers who will never come. In the harbour some ships are still burning.

The staff car broke down again in the middle of the afternoon and we finished our journey on a tow-rope. Camped near Magrun by an old roadhouse in the midst of wrecked tanks. Before midnight the Hun was shaking us around with heavy bombing.

Meanwhile No 250 Sqn had been informed that Flying Officers Miluck and Tribken were 'tour expired'. Its ORB for 10 December recorded: 'Fg Off Tribken and Fg Off Miluck leave us today on completion of tour'.

That was physically impossible, however, for when the news reached the squadron Ed Miluck was in the middle of the move from Martuba to Belandah. They seem to have stayed with 250, however, for another two weeks — though being shielded from any further operational flying, having done 200hr.

Ed Miluck and the four pilots with him reached the squadron's new landing-ground on 11 December:

Cleared Agedabia at 10 am. It was nothing but a cluster of mud buildings with a monument commemorating some glorious Italian victory over the native Senussi. Beyond it, the trip was tricky because land-mines were thickly sown, but we arrived at Belandah in time to watch the squadron go out on a bombing show.

This operation was described by No 239 Wing in its ORB:

> Wing Commander Haysom led a successful bombing attack on Nofilia aerodrome. This came after a long-range sweep over the area by 24 aircraft.

Ed Miluck's impressions of Belandah No 1 were not favourable:

> Again we are in the middle of nowhere, surrounded by nothing. This is one of the smallest, dustiest and rockiest landing-grounds we have yet been on. Every step means stumbling or twisting an ankle and the sides of our shoes are wearing out a hell of a lot faster than the soles. Water is so scarce that I hate to waste it even by sweating. Four of us share a tent, each one getting two pints of water daily. To stretch it we use our 'rotation ration' system, which involves a four-day period. Being first today, I took a cup of water and thoroughly washed my hands and face. When I had finished, Wally used the same cup of water to wash himself, then the other two had their turns. Mike Kelly was the last for washing, so he was the first for shaving, still using the same cup of water; and as I was first for washing, I was last for shaving. Our toilet completed, the cup of water was strained and put into another canteen kept for that purpose. When the canteen is full — two pints — it is my turn to take a bath, which means that we get a bath once every ten days. When I've finished bathing, the water is still mine to wash my clothes. After that, to hell with it — it's probably dirty, anyway.
>
> I remember, back in the States, when we used to take a nice, soapy bath in a tub full of hot water before going to bed. I remember washing luxuriously in foamy suds, gargling and rinsing out my mouth after brushing my teeth, then having a nice, fat yawn before going to bed. Now, before hitting the sack, I just wet my lips and pick my teeth.

He added, commenting on the operational situation:

> Learned that the army is going to hit the El Agheila line
> on the 14th and we will do our usual bombing and
> strafing. If we hit hard enough, there won't be anything
> between us and Tunis.

When the 8th Army had reached Benghazi, General
Rommel had — in the words of the RAF official historians[2] —
'reported to the Führer that the German motorized
formations in the forward area were completely immobile for
lack of petrol. A show of fight at El Agheila, however, saved
the German commander: the British troops deployed, and it
was not until mid-December that they swept into
Tripolitania...'.
El Agheila was a kind of El Alamein for the Axis forces and
Rommel had prepared his defences:

> By November 20, his army was there — minefields in
> position, stores brought down from a gutted Benghazi
> before final evacuation, left flank on the sea, right flank
> on the deep gorge of the Wadi Faregh; and on 12
> December, the British attacked the outposts after a heavy
> bombardment, drove them in and followed with a
> hesitancy and caution both extreme and apparent. Hopes
> and speculation arose in German breasts — had the
> British outrun their suppliers again? — and then one of
> the German recce 'planes spotted a column of almost 300
> vehicles sneaking past down south of the Wadi Faregh,
> and Rommel knew not only was his army being
> outfought, but also that he was being out-manoeuvred.
>   When 8th Army realised that Rommel was now pulling
> out of El Agheila, their last remaining doubts vanished.
> This time they were not to be sent reeling back; this time
> they were going forward to the end....[3]

On 13 December, No 239 Wing ORB recorded that
'throughout the day, fighter-bomber attacks were carried out

against enemy transport, mostly on the road west of Agheila'
— the Afrika Korps' withdrawal when they realized they
were being outflanked.

Ed Miluck put it much more bluntly in his diary for that
date:

> The bastards have done it again. They just won't fight.
> During the night, Rommel deserted El Agheila, leaving
> nothing but a lot of bloody mines. We're moving up to
> Marble Arch as soon as the roads are clear. Can't even
> strafe the galloping Hun because of the weather, and
> probably won't catch up with him again for a long time.

No 239 Wing started its move to the next landing-ground
on the afternoon of 14 December — although the move was
not to be completed for six days:

> 'B' party left at 1430hr to rendezvous with other units
> west of Agedabia, the intention being for a RAF convoy
> to proceed to Marble Arch immediately the road was
> cleared of mines. Air attacks on enemy MT were
> continued, and one Me109 was damaged when
> attempting to intercept our machines.

Not only were mines a problem; so was the weather — and
the food. Ed Miluck wrote on the 14th:

> The food has been so poor, we have considered eating
> Julius. He doesn't do much more than stink out the mess
> tent, anyway. For a week it's been canned bully, hot or
> cold, three times a day, with soupy cold tea and hard
> biscuits. When the rearguard catches up with us, there
> will maybe be a bit of stew, maybe a bit of marmalade or
> jam. The water is worse than the food — like drinking
> medicine, there is so much chlorine in it. Have been
> getting a little extra from a well down the road, but
> there's a dead Italian in it, so we don't use it for drinking
> — the Army does, though.

He reiterated the weather theme in his diary entry for 15 December, and touched on the means by which the Desert Air Force was to get over the problem of mined roads:

> Rain delayed our move again today, but we'll get out for sure tomorrow, moving the whole outfit by air this time to avoid mined roads. The Hun is getting further away than ever, and if we don't catch up in a couple of days we won't even be able to reach him by air.

The retreating enemy had not only mined the roads; they had ploughed-up the landing-grounds and liberally sprinkled them with booby-traps: even the most innocent-looking object was likely to conceal a lethal explosive charge. The real heroes at this time were the Army personnel who went forward to clear the LGs and make them usable — sometimes at a tragic cost to themselves:

> Twenty sappers were killed when clearing Marble Arch for 239 Wing. Not only the aerodrome, but all roads and approaches, were heavily mined. Hence air transport, which had been given a try-out for Operation Chocolate, was now to be used to move the entire Wing to its new site.[4]

It took two days (17–18 December) to accomplish the first part of this move, and two more for it to be completed. On the 17th, the Wing's ORB recorded: 'B' party left Agedabia with the RAF convoy, led by Wg Cdr Duncan of Advanced Air Headquarters, Western Desert, and travelled as far as Marsa Brega, where they spent the night'; then on the 18th: 'A Wing and Squadron party, known as 'B Plus' party, was transported to Marble Arch by air, and all aircraft flew there to commence operations, which once more consisted of bombing and strafing enemy transport. 'B' party reached a point five miles from Marble Arch'.

Ed Miluck described this airlift in his diary entry for 16 December, his dates not quite coinciding with those of the No

239 Wing ORB, but his description adding considerable detail:

> Marble Arch, Mussolini's gateway to the Italian resort land, is just a marble arch and nothing more[5]. Our entire personnel and equipment arrived on schedule by 'plane — a remarkable feat and a triumph for modern air warfare. As Jerry had mined the landing-grounds and ploughed them up — a sure sign he doesn't intend to return — the Army made us an airfield in half a day's time with a couple of road-scrapers. Since this is the most advanced base, it has more traffic than La Guardia.
>
> Our tents are set in a series of small ravines a mile away, and if there were only something to see besides sand, it would be quite pleasant. Effective drainage anyway. The Army put on a good show yesterday. Cut off some of Jerry's rearguard with a flanking movement and messed it up quite a bit.

But the *Luftwaffe* took its revenge under cover of darkness. On the 17th he wrote:

> They really pasted us last night! — never have so few been bombed by so many, with so much, for so long a time. Never have I seen such heavy bombing. It wasn't so bad at first, but the raid got worse and worse. Every time a bomb whistled down my heart missed several beats, until it landed; then they began coming down so fast that my heart began doing a kind of skipping-rope to keep up: I guess the Gremlins[6] turned the rope. My mouth was so dry that my chewing-gum rolled around like a chalk marble in a paper box. I thought it might help if I put in another stick — but no good, so I put all five in. Every time a bomb fell, my head shook; and every time my head shook, it sounded like a crap game. Talk about an empty feeling in the pit of your stomach! — What stomach?

No 250 Sqn was in action again on the 18th, in pursuit of the retreating Afrika Korps — 'a long-range strafe, with destruction of a large number of trucks moving along the road ahead'. But these latter December days proved disastrous for the Kittyhawk squadrons — particularly No 250. No 239 Wing recorded on the 20th: 'Three pilots are missing from patrols over our forward troops'; and on the same date Ed Miluck wrote in his diary:

> Unhappy 250 Squadron lost four pilots the day before yesterday and two more today, as well as several 'planes damaged in landing.
> The first four broke away from the squadron to attack a lone Me109 stooging below as sucker bait — and, of course, Heinrich and his friends were waiting in the sun for just such a manoeuvre. The aerial combat covered half of Africa and ended-up with an even score — but that doesn't replace the aircraft or the pilots.
> The second pair just got tangled up in another dogfight, and when that happens, somebody always plays a little rough and somebody else always gets hurt.

On 21 December, No 239 Wing recorded further ground-attack operations and the beginning of another move westwards:

> Patrols were carried out, and the landing-ground at Hun was attacked, seven enemy aircraft being destroyed and three damaged on the ground. In the air, one Me109 was damaged. 'B' party proceeded to a point one mile west of Nofilia landing-ground.

Ed Miluck made a brief reference to these operations in his diary: 'Two long-range strafes today, both baksheesh. No enemy 'planes, very little ack-ack.'

Then on the 22nd he noted:

Paddy Cairns brought our beer and Christmas supplies today from Alexandria in a captured Heinkel 111. He has finished his operational hours and is due for a rest, so they offered him this job.

The two Americans on No 250 (Sudan) Sqn had also finished their operational tours; and on 23 December Ed Miluck made a last entry in the desert in the diary he had kept since the beginning of October 1942:

Tonight the drinks are on the commanding officer, Wally [Tribken] and me. Our good fortune is that we have done better than 200 combat hours and are still alive. We have been recalled to Cairo for reassignment to a non-combat area for a few months, probably as instructors at a boring Operational Training Unit. Goodbye, 250 Squadron! Farewell to the Hun!

Notes to Chapter 9

1   These were Italian colonists, settled in Tripolitania and Cyrenaica as part of Mussolini's attempt to recreate the Roman Empire.
2   *Royal Air Force 1939–1945 Vol II The Fight Avails,* by Denis Richards and Hilary St George Saunders (HMSO).
3   From *The Chase to Tunisia,* by Barrie Pitt, in *The Sunday Times Book of El Alamein and the Desert War* (Sphere Books Ltd, 1967).
4   *The Desert Air Force,* by Roderic Owen (Hutchinson). Operation Chocolate was the positioning of two Hurricane squadrons, Nos 213 and 238, on LG125 — about 180 miles east of Agedabia — on 13 November. From there they had attacked retreating enemy columns, taking them completely by surprise.
5   This gleaming white arch straddled the Tripoli–Benghazi coastal road. Around it, as in Shelley's sonnet *Ozymandias* '....boundless and bare/The lone and level sands stretch far away.'
6   A Gremlin was a mythical wartime creature upon whom all unaccountable troubles were blamed.

CHAPTER 10
Two Ways to Cairo — from the East and from the West

On the same date — 23 December 1942 — a first entry was being made by Hal Marting in the dark blue pocket-diary he bought in Konya, Turkey, on the 24th. Like Ed Miluck, he had been an inveterate diary-keeper and quickly resumed the habit in his early days of freedom after his escape from the Germans in Athens and his months of evasion through the mountainous Greek countryside. His entries were to show that getting to Cairo from Western Turkey brought out in him the same kind of determination he had shown in his pre-Desert Air Force days, in his nearly three months' service with No 450 Squadron and during two months as a PoW and fugitive. On the 23rd he wrote (when they were probably at Izmir, though he is not specific about the starting point of their journey):

> Up at 0600hr this morning to pack and breakfast. Van Witten, the Intelligence Officer, came for us in two taxis at 0730. We all have British passports.
> The train pulled out at 0830. We have a 2nd Class compartment to ourselves but it is very cramped and cold. We are all suffering from the cold. Had all our meals in the car from the big bag of food we took with us — boiled eggs, meat balls, bread and various fruits and nuts. Mrs Puleins, the hostess of the guest house, also gave us a cake for our Christmas.

On Christmas Eve he recounted their slow journey through the mountainous Turkish countryside:

> What a miserable night! We arrived at Afyon at 0300hr this morning, cold, stiff and hungry. Had a meal of hot soup, cheese and two eggs and beer in the railway café

and went to sleep afterwards sitting at the table. It was very crowded and the air foul but warm.

Our train finally arrived at 0730. We rushed out and managed to get in the first-class car, but there are not enough seats for us, so some must be standing all the time. We are warm now and much more comfortable. Got acquainted with an officer of the Turkish Army who is in our compartment. He can speak no English, or anything but Turkish, so we hardly understand each other.

At Konya we had a stop for an hour and we had a short walk trying to find some matches, but found none. Bought some Turkish candy and this diary. During our walk the Turk slapped several soldiers and kicked one very hard — all for very trivial things. Quite different here!

There was snow and thick frost everywhere today, which seems out of place here. I feel sorry for the poor peasants here, who walk about with very inadequate clothes — some barefooted. But they are much nearer being animals than humans.

Hal Marting headed his next entry 'Dec 25 — Friday — Xmas':

After a very miserable night, which we spent trying to keep each other warm, we arrived at Adana just before dawn. The heating was turned off during the night and it was very cold. We have crossed the southern range of mountains and the country here is more beautiful.

We bought cigarettes, matches and chocolate and drank lots of hot milk, so we feel much better now.

We spent almost all of our time today playing 'Pontoon' and I won about £4 sterling.

Arrived at Pasa, Turkey, at about 1400hr and there changed trains for the last lap into British territory. Finally got across the border after the officials had fooled around for an hour or so — crossing at about 1530hr. Arrived at Maydanekbez, the first frontier post of the

British, at about 1800hr. Had a beer there and bought some biscuits and dates and went on to Aleppo, where we arrived at about 2330hr.

We were supposed to go to a transit camp, but fortunately they could get no transportation for us, so we came to hotels. Four of us are here in the Claridge.

My feet are still pretty sore and my ankles swollen.

So much for Christmas Day (which happened to be the first day back in Cairo for Miluck and Tribken). On Boxing Day, some complications occurred:

Woke rather early this morning and had a shave and a wonderful hot bath. Max[1] and I had a double breakfast each.

The truck came for us at 0930hr and we were taken to an Army office where the other members of the party had spent the night, not being able to find any rooms in the hotels. They had had no breakfast. About 10 o'clock an Army Captain arrived and told us he would return in a few minutes and take the fellows out to breakfast.

We waited for two hours and nothing happened, so I left the fellows with Max and walked to the British Consulate to try to get enough money to buy them something to eat. I told the Consul of our peculiar reception and he was quite angry about it. He 'phoned the Captain (Donaldson), who said that he had been making arrangements for the breakfast, which was not true at all.

There was an army Colonel in the office who had heard my complaint and who was very sympathetic about the whole thing. He suggested that Max and I go with him in his car to a mobile hospital to have our feet dressed and I accepted. Captain Donaldson arrived then and Max and the others also arrived in a truck. As the Colonel and I went out of the office we passed Donaldson, who gave me a very dirty look.

We picked up Max and went on to the hospital and got our feet bandaged. We had a drink with the doctor and the Colonel sent his car back for us to take us to join the others. We did not find them so waited at Captain Donaldson's office. He 'phoned in at about 1700hr and told us to report to the Provost Marshal.

We walked over there and they took us in a truck to find Donaldson. He was not in his office so I said, 'To hell with this, we can go back to the hotel for lunch.' The lance-corporal who had brought us said that we could not do that as we were *under arrest!* Max and I were both very indignant about this and I refused to be arrested, on the ground that there was no officer senior to me who had placed me under arrest. The corporal asked if we would go back to the Provost Marshal's office with him while he found out what to do, so we agreed.

There we met a Lt Markham who is looking after us while here, and he tells me that we are under open arrest, but that no charge has been placed. Indeed, none can be, as we have violated no orders or regulations.

We were taken with the others out to a disinfecting centre to have ourselves and our clothes disinfected, and had lunch and tea there. Came back into town about 1800hr with Max. He had to give some information to the Intelligence Officers, and while waiting for him I saw Donaldson, but he didn't say anything to me at all. Max and I are spending the night in the Claridge again. All the others have to stay at the disinfecting place.

On 27 December they at last got away from Aleppo:

We had breakfast in bed this morning and then went out for a short walk and bought some magazines to read on the train. We are to leave at 2208 tonight on a sleeper train.

They took us out to a barracks and issued us uniforms for the rest of the journey. I am fitted out in Australian Army Service dress now and my Air Force stripes look very peculiar. It is very warm though, and we now have gloves and greatcoats, which are a big help.

Had lunch at the hotel and this afternoon Max and I went to a movie. Back at the hotel there was a message waiting for us to call the Consulate. The British Consul invited us up to dinner and came for us in his car at 1800hr. We had a very nice meal at the Consulate and he then took us to the train, which left at 1950hr instead of the later hour. The train was heated but the 'sleepers' were myths.

On the 28th they reached Damascus after their overnight journey.

Arrived at some small town at about 0800hr where we changed trains for Damascus — which we got to at about 1400hr and spent the afternoon trying to extract some money from the Pay Office, finally wangling £5 sterling.

Max and I are staying at the Hotel Orion, which is very modern and comfortable and the food fine. Bought a knife of Damascus steel, an ivory carving and some photos of this famous city.

Went to a night club after dinner and got plastered. To bed at 0100hr.

Despite 'the night before', they had to make a very early start from Damascus:

Had to get up at 0600hr to catch our train. Don't feel too well even after a bath. Took train for Haifa at 0800hr. The ride was very tiresome and there was very little scenery to look at. Arrived at Haifa at 2200hr and put up at the Savoy, a very modern hotel. Had supper at the Officers' Club before going to bed.

They spent the morning of 30 December in Haifa, replenishing their finances and doing some more shopping:

Got up at 0800hr and after breakfast went to Barclays and got a cheque cashed for £10. Bought some souvenirs, a camera and film, and had a shave and haircut. Had lunch at the Savoy and boarded the train for Cairo at 1345hr.

This train is much better and goes at a good speed. It is much warmer down here, too. Played 'Pontoon' most of the afternoon.

The very last entry in Hal Marting's dark-blue Turkish pocket diary is a very brief one, for 31 December 1942:

We stopped for breakfast at Lydda at about 0300hr and arrived at Cairo at 0830hr. Max and I and the officer escorting us found a room at the National for tonight.

He was not to know that he would have a reunion that night with some old friends from No. 239 Wing who had arrived in the city on 24 December — 'in time', as Ed Miluck put it in his diary after their flight back from the desert, 'for a hot shower and a shave before Christmas Eve dinner — a sumptuous feast of the tenderest turkey imaginable'.

On the 28th Ed Miluck recorded another reunion:

Glad to see Lance Wade, another American in the RAF (DFC and Bar)[2] in the Continental Savoy, just returned from the States after six weeks' leave. Listened to him with rapture, remembering that I haven't seen the States in two years.

On the evening of the following day he 'had dinner at Shepheard's Hotel as the guest of Major M.C. Beil, USAAF Medical Corps, and through his good efforts was able to contact Mother'. Then the very last entry in his diary, for New Year's Eve 1942, recorded ecstatically the best reunion of all — with the long-lost friend with whom he had joined the Desert Air Force — and also his own posting, and that of Wally Tribken, to the United States for transfer to the USAAF:

Yippee! Marting walked in this evening, very casually, as if he had just been out for a drink — when, in truth, he had just escaped from the Germans in Greece. What a New Year's Eve. What a ....

More good news! Heap big smoke signal, hot from under the blanket. Wally and I are transferred to the US Army Air Corps[3] and are being sent to the States immediately.

Home.
We're still alive.
We're going HOME ....

Notes to Chapter 10

1 Max is the only fellow escaper/evader whom Hal Marting identifies by name.
2 Lance Wade had a remarkable operational career in the Desert Air Force, winning the DFC and Bar and the DSO. Tragically, he was then killed in a flying accident in Italy.
3 The US Army Air Corps became the USAAF (US Army Air Force) in 1941.

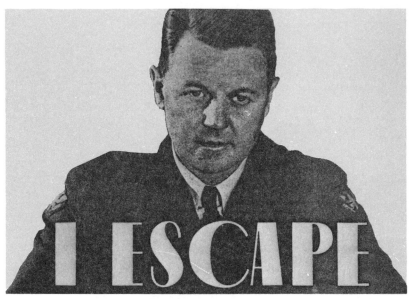

The title page of Hal Marting's article in *The American Magazine*, August 1943 issue.

Wally Tribken in mid-1942 — a Cairo studio photograph. Sadly, he was killed in a jeep accident in Belgium in 1944.

Marting's Military Cross with (above it) the 'winged boot' symbol of the Late Arrivals Club — awarded to those aircrew who were shot down and successfully made their way back to their squadrons.

Epilogue

HAL MARTING was also sent to the United States — in his case, repatriated. He was still a Flying Officer in the RCAF, from which he was discharged on medical grounds early in 1943: the physical privations which he had endured during the escape/evasion in Greece had taken their toll — his feet were still damaged and he was suffering from scurvy, due to a lack of Vitamin C through a shortage of proper food and vegetables. However, he made a good recovery and got back into flying as a civilian pilot — with Curtiss-Wright Corporation, makers of the P-40 Kittyhawk which he flew in the Desert Air Force.

On 14 July 1943 he was awarded the Military Cross — a rare award for an American. The citation said simply:

> The King has been graciously pleased to approve the following award in recognition of gallant and distinguished service:
>
> Military Cross
>
> Flying Officer Harold Fesler Marting RCAF, No 450 (RAAF) Sqn.

A biographical note accompanying the citation said:

> 'Flying Officer Marting RCAF was born in 1911 in Indiana, USA. His home is at Indianapolis, Ind. He served as Corporal in the US Marine Corps from 1927 to 1931. He enlisted in the RAF in 1940, training in Canada under the Joint Air Training Plan. He was commissioned in the Special Reserve in 1941 as a pilot.'

No mention was made of his escape from PoW captivity and his subsequent successful evasion, and there is no report of his experiences in RAF archives. Normally, RAF personnel who successfully evaded recapture were interrogated on their return and their reports filed. Bound volumes of these — containing some of the most daring and courageous exploits of the Second World War — are held in the Air Historical Branch (RAF) of the Ministry of Defence. But there is no report on Flying Officer H.F. Marting's escape from Athens and subsequent evasion, with the help of the Greek Resistance. The main account which exists is that written by Hal Marting himself and published in *The American Magazine* for August 1943, and which has been used in this book. But it is a censored account, reduced from an original 10,000 to 6,000 words, the aim being to protect the identity of Marting's brave helpers. No doubt he would have written a fuller version after the war and their bravery would have been officially recognized.

But there was to be no 'after the war' for Hal Marting. His flying with Curtiss-Wright involved being co-pilot of a Curtiss C-46 Commando used by the company on goodwill tours. There is a photograph of him — probably one of the last ones taken — with eight of his colleagues in front of the C-46, named *Gremlin's Castle*, published in the company newspaper, *The Curtiss Wright-ER*, dated 13 August 1943.

Just over a month later, on 20 September, he was flying a P-40 back to Buffalo after a goodwill tour, with some photographs he was anxious to deliver to Eastman Kodak at Rochester, New York.

When he made a refuelling stop at Tifton Air Field, Georgia, he was urged not to take off again because of storms to the north — but he decided to 'press on'. At Bishopville, South Carolina, his aircraft flew into the ground and he was killed. Whether he was attempting to get 'under the weather' and hit a hill, or was trying to make a forced-landing, will never be known.

Ed Miluck was then with 403 Fighter Group, Drew Field, Tampa, Florida, and Hal's sister Lenore (Mrs Don Silvers) got into touch with him 'at the last moment' (to quote from a letter of hers)

> and he flew up for the funeral, taking a 'plane he had never flown before, getting into bad weather on the way

and in general risking his life to get here. He was too late for the funeral, but he stayed overnight, met Mother and Dad, and we all love him for coming.

This was a farewell salute from one Desert Eagle to another, for the last time Hal Marting and Ed Miluck had been on operations together was in No 239 Wing, Desert Air Force, on 23 October 1942 — just before the start of the Battle of El Alamein.

In 1946 there was another posthumous salute to Hal Marting — from Greece, when Mrs Angela Melidi wrote to his sister on 12 March, enclosing a diary he had kept while in Athens and asking for news of him[1]:

> Perhaps my name is known to you, perhaps not. In any case I feel a holy duty to write these lines and send the journal of your brother Harold Marting, who was captured by Germans and hospitalized by me in Athens after having escaped, as you will learn from the details from the enclosed journal[2].
>
> Dear Madam, I have already written to him, but unfortunately till now I have not his news and write to me if he is in good health because I consider him as my adopted brother since we passed many troubles together during his stay in Athens.
>
> I am very happy to be able to send this journal to you. This was his wish, and please answer to me as soon as you receive this letter.

* * * * *

ED MILUCK served in the USAAF from 3 January 1943 to 15 May 1946, rising to the rank of Major, having graduated from the Command and General Staff School in 1945 and having in his active Service career — in Europe and North Africa — flown 110 combat missions. In September 1947 he changed his first name from Edward to Michael and he remained in the Reserves until 1957. During the late 1940s and 1950s he established Stinson Field Aero, a flying school and maintenance base in San Antonio, Texas, exporting aircraft to Latin America. He also graduated from Cornell University School of Hotel and Restaurant Management, a qualification which served him well. For when he was called up by the USAF in 1951 during the Korean conflict he was transferred from operational duties to complete his tour as manager of all USAF-leased hotels and officers' clubs in Tokyo.

Michael Miluck then started a new career — theatrical film sales and production, which took him for two years to London, Paris and Rome, then back to the United States — where he settled into restaurant management in San Francisco. There, in 1964, he married Nancy Christian and in the following year became involved in a new line of activity — restoring a three-storey, 12-roomed 1887 house. The Milucks' first daughter, Mary Grace, was born in San Francisco in 1966.

Three years later they moved to Genoa, Nevada's first settlement and just across the Sierras from Lake Tahoe, and in 1970 increased its population from about 116 to 117 when their second daughter Elizabeth Christian (Elise) was born.

Having settled into the country to continue research on myths, fables and legends for a proposed television series conceived originally in 1954, Michael Miluck — with Nancy's aid — compiled a book on Genoa to raise funds for a TV translator system for the area, supervising this from its inception through its incorporation to its operation.

He still continues to do house restoration – now a family enterprise — and has many a Victorian dwelling to his credit; he is also a gifted writer and illustrator of children's stories and he and Nancy are involved in a small publishing company which issues the *Genoa–Carson Valley Book* every few years and has published a history of Nevada.

Michael Miluck is a member of the Eagle Squadrons' Association, which in 1991 celebrated its 50th anniversary; and his Second World War diary of his days in the Desert Air Force with Hal Marting, Wally Tribken and their fellow Americans has contributed substantially to this book — as has correspondence with, and material and photographs supplied by, the ever-enthusiastic and helpful Nancy Miluck.

Notes to Epilogue

1 This letter is reproduced in the recent book (previously mentioned) by the late Vern Haugland, *Caged Eagles: Downed American Fighter Pilots 1940–45* (TAB Aero, Blue Ridge Summit, PA 17294–0850). His book *The Eagle Squadrons — Yanks in the RAF 1940–1942* (Ziff-Davies Flying Books) was published in 1979.
2 A journal not, unfortunately, made available to the author of this book.

Glossary of Terms

AA, anti-aircraft fire
CFS, Central Flying School
EFTS, Elementary Flying Training School
ITS, Initial Training School
LG, landing gear
MET, mechanised enemy transport
MT, motor transport
ORB, Operations Record Book
OTU, Operational Training Unit
PTC, Personnel Transit Unit
SFS, Service Flying School
WO, Warrant Officer
W/T, wireless telegraphy

Index

Montgomery, Field Marshal Viscount,
  48, 83
Msus, 106, 107, 108
Myles, Gladys, 5

National Hotel, 129
Nevada, 134
New Zealand Club, 27, 29, 31, 35, 39
Nile Delta, 1
North Dakota, 1
Nubariya Canal, 27

O'Berg, W., 59
O'Brien, Pat, 112
Operation Chocolate, 120, 123fn
Operation Supercharge, 79
Operation Torch, 96fn
Orion Hotel, 128

Palestine, 52fn
Pasa, 125
Port Sudan, 51fn
Puleins, Mrs, 124
Pyramids, 10, 44

Qattara, 18
Qattara Afrem, 18
Qattara Depression, 18, 52fn, 65

RAF/RAAF/RCAF/RNZAF/SAAF
  personnel (ranks as at first mention):
  Bangs, Sqn Ldr, 3; Barber, Flt Lt
  M.C.H., 65, 79fn, 89; Barclay, Sqn Ldr
  R.G.A., 11fn; Baron, Sgt, 73; –
  Bicksler, E., 114fn
  Cairns, Plt Off D.W., 41, 47, 54fn, 103,
  122; Calver, Fg Off, 73, 87, 88;
  Carsons, Flt Lt W., 16; Chap, Sgt N.R.,
  87, 88; Clark, Flt Lt, 45; Clouse, Sqn
  Ldr, 109; Collier, Plt Off, 18, 101;
  Coningham, AVM A., 37, 40, 41, 53fn,
  83
  Davidson, Sgt, 19; Devenish, Sqn Ldr,
  24; Donald, Plt Off, 52fn; Duncan, Wg
  Cdr, 120; Dyson, Flt Sgt R.D., 19, 29,
  52fn
  Edwards, W.O., 18; Evans, Sgt, 47;
  Ewing, Sgt, 30, 53fn
  Falconer-Taylor, Plt Off J.R., 46, 54fn,
  63; Ferguson, Sqn Ldr A.D., 19, 31, 37,
  47, 52fn; Forneau, Sgt, 73; 'Freddie',
  –., 101
  Graham, Flt Sgt, 73; Gregory, –., 45
  Hancock, Flt Lt –., 18, 65, 73, 77, 89,
  105, 109; Haysom, Wg Cdr, G.D.L.,

18, 22, 31, 37, 51fn, 62, 106, 117;
Holloway, Sgt –., 38; Holmes, Flt Sgt
–., 40, 47, 58, 101, 105
Judd, Sqn Ldr M.T., 47, 77, 84, 93, 108,
109
Kelly, Fg Off M., 2, 6, 7, 10, 11fn, 12,
117
Law, Flt Sgt –., 19; Law, Plt Off –., 29;
Law, Sqn Ldr D., 48, 49; Lindsey, Sgt
–., 47
Mannix, Sqn Ldr R.L., 9, 11fn, 21, 22,
28, 36, 53fn, 110fn, 114; Marble, Sgt –.,
25; Martin, Sgt –., 78; Marting, Fg Off
H.F., 1 and passim; Matthews, Flt Lt
–., 28, 40, 53fn; Miluck, Fg Off E.T., 1
and passim
McBurnie, Flt Sgt D.H., 19, 29, 52fn;
MacFarlane, Sgt –., 31, 32
Newton, –.–., 105; Nitz, Sgt –., 87, 105;
Nomis, Plt Off L., 31, 44, 53fn
Oakley, Sgt –., 28; O'Brien, Flt Sgt –.,
87; O'Neil, Sgt –., 30
Parker, Flt Lt –., 27; Pegge, Sqn Ldr
C.O.J., 21, 52fn; Phelps, Sgt –., 29;
Phillips, –. 'Tex', 95; Plinston, –.–.,
105; Prowse, –.–., 45
Roberts, Flt Sgt, A.E., 45; Rodney, Flt
Sgt –., 38; Russel, Plt Off –., 18, 87
Scaaf, Plt Off –., 19, 33; Scribner, Sgt
–., 52fn; Sheppard, Flt Sgt –., 29;
Shepperd, Flt Lt Mc R., 40, 53fn;
Shillabeer, Plt Off N.H., 24, 52fn; Sly,
Plt Off E.L., 22, 28, 52fn; Stephens, Sgt
–., 73; Stewart, Plt Off –., 66, 105;
Strausan, Sqn Ldr –., 104; Strong, Sgt
–., 53fn
Taylor, Fg Off –., 18, 73, 105; Taylor,
Sgt R.C., 28, 46; Tedder, AM Sir A.,
22, 67; Terry, Sqn Ldr –., 104; Thorpe,
Plt Off –., 53fn; Trenchard, MRAF
Lord, 36, 42, 53fn; Tribken, Fg Off W.,
2, 4, 6, 7, 8, 10, 11fn, 12, 15, 17, 19, 20,
22, 24, 25, 26, 28, 32, 37, 38, 44, 46, 62,
93, 111, 113, 114, 117, 123, 129, 134;
Troke, Plt Off G.W., 44, 54fn, 87, 88,
90, 105; Tyson, Wg Cdr –., 3
Upward, Fg Off J.W., 22, 52fn
Wade, Wg Cdr L., 129, 130fn; Ward,
–.R.C., 21, 52fn; Whiteside, Plt Off –.,
18, 73; Williams, Flt Lt –., 28;
Williams, Sqn Ldr J.E.A., 47, 74;
Wilmot, Col –., 5; Wilson, –.P., 4;
Winn, Plt Off –., 40, 45; Wright, Plt
Off –., 77
Young, Sgt –., 52fn

RAF stations:
Kirton-in-Lindsey, 2; Padgate 24
RAF/RAAF/SAAF squadrons:
Nos 2 (SAAF), 51fn, 94; 3 (RAAF), 12,
14, 15, 23, 24, 27, 29, 38, 44, 46, 47,
52fn; 4 (SAAF), 51fn; 5 (SAAF), 51fn;
14, 54fn; 33, 11fn, 110fn; 71, 2, 31, 32,
52fn, 53fn; 92, 53fn; 112, 12, 14, 22, 29,
33, 58, 62, 65, 72, 73, 79, 88, 95; 117,
96fn; 121, 2, 52fn; 127, 9, 52fn; 114;
173, 96fn; 213, 123fn; 216, 96fn; 229,
53fn; 238, 123fn; 250 (Sudan), 14 and
passim; 260, 51fn; 267, 96fn; 450
(RAAF), 12 and *passim*; 462 (RAAF),
53fn; 601, 11fn, 109
RAF units:
AAHQ (Advanced Air
Headquarters), 17; Nos 56 and 59
OTUs, 2; No 21 PTC, 9; No 22 PTC,
10; No 233 Wing, 51fn, 90, 96; No 239
Wing, 12 and *passim*
Ras Al Kanayis, 48
Ras El Alam El Rum, 65
Red Cross, Int, 76
Red Sea, 6, 8
Regina, 1
Rommel, Generalfeldmarschall, 6, 84,
118

San Antonio, 2
San Francisco, 134
Santa Maria, 2
Savoy Hotel, 128, 129
Seattle, 59
Senussi, 116
Shelley, P.B., 123
Shepheard's Hotel, 9, 129
Sheridan, Ann, 112
Ships:
HMS *Derbyshire*, 1; SS *Harperley*, 52fn;
SS *Aorangi*, 1, 2, 4; HMTs *Georgic*, 1;
Mauretania, 11fn; *Nieuw Amsterdam*, 5,
6, 7, 8
Sicily, 67
Sidi Barrani, 60, 74, 78, 83, 87, 90, 94
Sidi El Rahman, 42
Sidi Haneish, 40
Silvers, Mrs D., 72, 132
Smuts, FM J.C., 4
Snyder, Lt Col A.W., 26, 52fn
Sollum, 87, 88, 90, 93, 94
South Africa, 1
Stalingrad, 52fn
Stardust Night Club, 4
Stinson Field Aero, 134

Suez, 8, 9

Ta Kali, 53fn
Takoradi, 51fn
Tampa, 59
Tifton airfield, 132
Tobruk, 40, 59, 60, 94, 95, 96, 102
Tocra, 100
Tokyo, 134
Trenton, 1
Tripoli, 89, 111
Tripolitania, 118
Troy, 36, 97
Tunis, 89, 118
Turkey, 68, 124
Turkish Army, 125

Ulysses, 97
USAAF units:
81st, 82nd, 83rd and 434th Sqns, 12th
Bdt Gp, 52fn
Command & General Staff School,
133
64th Ftr Sqn, 57th Ftr Gp, 33, 54fn;
65th Ftr Sqn, 94; 66th Ftr Sqn, 32, 33,
40, 44, 46, 53fn, 54fn, 58
403 Ftr Gp, 132
US Army Air Corps, 1, 2, 10, 130fn
US Army Air Force, 2, 35, 31
US Independence Day, 7
US Legation
US Marine Corps, 131
US Marines, 1
US Navy, 15, 41

Vancouver, 1
Van Witten, 134
Very, S.W., 101
Volkswagen, 56

Wadi Faregh, 118
Wadi Natrun, 12
Warrington, 52fn
Weir, Lt J., 21
Wellington House, 10, 14, 15, 16, 20, 22,
31, 32, 36, 39
West African Reinforcement Route, 51fn
Western Desert, 12 and *passim*
Williams, Ike, 4
Wilson, Pat, 4
Windsor, Ont., 1
Windsor Palace Hotel, 21
Wynn, H., 1fn

Yemen , 8